You Can Move MOUNTAINS

A Story of a Mother and Her Daughter

CAROL NORRIS

and

KELSEY ANASTASIA NORRIS

ISBN 978-1-0980-2918-0 (paperback)
ISBN 978-1-0980-2919-7 (digital)

Christian Faith Publishing, Inc.
832 Park Avenue
Meadville, PA 16335
www.christianfaithpublishing.com

Cover photo credit: Bonnie Rebholz

Printed in the United States of America

CHAPTER 1

My Business and Life
Before Kelsey

I came to Georgia in June 1986 after I had just graduated with a master's degree in health administration from Washington University School of Medicine in St. Louis, Missouri. I had never lived in the South and had only been to Georgia on one previous trip to interview for the full-time administrative fellowship position at St. Joseph's Hospital in Savannah. I knew no one in the state and had no support system. I was a first-generation college graduate who had big dreams about using my education to make a difference in the world.

When I drove into Savannah, I only had a couple hundred dollars in my bank account, a very large student loan debt and a car with an almost empty gas tank. I furnished a small one-bedroom apartment with a folding table, a folding chair, a small bed (that looked like a cot), and two chairs and a love seat that I bought at a garage sale for $30. The fellowship only paid $14,000 per year, so money was tight that first year in Savannah. I learned how to live on eating one meal every couple of days. It wasn't that bad because I lost fifty pounds during my first few months there. Thankfully, some of the department managers and other hospital staff members invited me to their houses to have dinner and meet their families. I met and became friends with many wonderful people who taught me a great deal about the health care industry and the dedicated people who care for the sick and injured. It was rewarding to be helping people and to be learning how to make a difference in the world.

Being an administrative fellow at the hospital taught me much more about the competitive and ruthless side of the health care industry. After I finished my fellowship, I accepted the full-time position of assistant to the president and stayed in Savannah for six years. By the end of the six years, I had learned much about how the decisions that the executives and insurance companies make impact patients' lives. I witnessed what poor leadership can do to an organization and to the community it serves. This poor leadership included an inadequate CEO and ineffective board oversight.

I was beginning to wonder why some CEOs could sleep at night knowing that the decisions they made during the day were going to negatively impact so many lives. It was especially disillusioning for me when I would subsequently have to interact with employees, patients, and community members knowing and remaining silent regarding the fact that my boss had done so much to diminish their quality of life. Most of the time, they had no idea what had been said about them or how their life was going to be changed in the future. I came to the realization that being a CEO carries a great deal of responsibility. I am not just talking about financial responsibility. More importantly, I am talking about the responsibility to be ethnical and honest and put the employees and patients first. Not every CEO has that mind-set. I could write an entire book on this subject but that will have to wait for another time (my next book).

*****

In October 1994, I had the opportunity to interview for a very exciting position in Atlanta. The Georgia Hospital Association, in partnership with the Georgia Departments of Human Resources and Medical Assistance, was implementing a demonstration project called the Community Decision Making Program. The program was going to work with ten rural underserved counties in Georgia. The project's purpose was to mobilize community members regarding health care planning and decision-making in order to generate long-term support for the local health care infrastructure. I interviewed for the state coordinator position and was offered the job. It was a wonderful opportunity to make a difference in some of Georgia's poorest and most medically underserved counties. I loved that position and loved working with the dedicated individuals from those counties.

I had worked for a health care consultant while I had been a graduate student in St. Louis and had enjoyed the environment of being able to work on a variety of projects in several different states, so I understood what successful consultants do. While working as the state coordinator for the Georgia Community Decision Making Program, I realized how much I liked working in the individual counties on specific projects. After much thought and prayer, I decided that I was being called by the Lord to start my own consulting business. After approximately eighteen months serving as the state coordinator, I announced my resignation and stayed to train my replacement. After training my replacement, I left that position and immediately started working on projects as a consultant. The first project I had was to coordinate an eight-month maternal and child health project for the State Medical Education Board of Georgia, Georgia Department of Medical Assistance and Mercer University School of Medicine. After that, other state offices such as the state's children's health director and children's medical services contracted with me.

I worried during this transition that I might be making a big career mistake and that I would not be able to find enough work as a consultant. However, that was not the case. Public health districts, hospitals, county school systems, and community collaboratives throughout the state started contacting me, asking if I was available to assist them on projects. Most of the projects involved community needs assessments, strategic planning, resource development, evaluation, and grant writing.

During these past twenty-five years, I have never been happier and more fulfilled. I love what I do and it shows. I have had the opportunity to work for some of the best people in Georgia. During the past several years, I have assisted clients prepare over three hundred successfully funded grant proposals totaling over $153 million. This funding has helped them serve hundreds of thousands of the most at-risk children and youth in the state and their families. This funding has empowered these organizations to develop school-based health centers; delinquency prevention initiatives; school-based mental health services; child health networks; substance abuse prevention initiatives; school nurse services; school wellness programs; early childhood development initiatives; community-based teen pregnancy prevention activities; chronic disease case management programs; developmental after school enrichment opportunities that promote academic achievement, leadership development, employment skills, and future career goals; family support and case management activities; HIV/AIDS services; senior citizen health screening initiatives; employer wellness initiatives; county and statewide health outreach initiatives; statewide health screening programs; and integrated health care computer (technology) infrastructure systems.

*****

Because of my expertise, I have also conducted workshops and provided technical assistance on a variety of health, social, and educational issues at the local, state, and national level. I have been able to conduct national resource development and grant writing seminars which have trained over five thousand individuals from throughout the country. I have also conducted statewide, regional, and local strategic planning and related needs assessment processes and designed comprehensive strategic plans and ongoing evaluation processes for individual organizations, as well as over seventy grassroots community collaboratives. In addition, I currently publish a monthly resource development e-newsletter that has over 3,500 individuals/ organizations from throughout the United States and several foreign countries on its distribution list.

*****

Starting my own consulting business was not easy. It took every ounce of my determination and energy to make my business success-ful. There were some years, in the beginning, that I worked 365 days straight (with no time off for weekends and holi-days), only pausing to go to church on Sunday. My workdays were all at least—twelve to sixteen hours long and I spent at least three to four days every week on the road staying at hotels. Georgia is a big state and, at some point, I have worked on projects in most of the 159 counties.

Figure 1 Norris Consulting Group office

I achieved my goals by focusing like a laser beam on my business and my clients. By 2002, my company was recognized as one of the leading consultants (specializing in health, social service, and educa-tion-related projects) in the United States. We not only write success-ful grant proposals, but we also evaluate the effectiveness of projects after they are implemented. One day, in 2002, I stopped to eat lunch at a Cracker Barrel on the four-hour drive back to my office from a client meeting. While I was eating my lunch, I looked around and saw families eating together with their children. Something clicked in my heart while I was watching the parents interact with their chil-dren. I thought to myself that this must be how the rest of the world lives. At that time, I was forty-two years old and I always had thought that by the time I was forty-two, I would be married and raising chil-dren as a working mom. I realized that time was marching on, and I began thinking that I was at a decision point in my life.

Adopting Kelsey

Later that year, I was in Kansas City at a national Safe Schools/ Healthy Students conference with Carolyn Swint, who is a friend and client. While we were at lunch, I told Carolyn Swint that I had been thinking about adoption for the past couple of years, but I did not know where to begin. She suggested that I talk to the assistant superintendent at her school system because she has two granddaughters who had been adopted from a Russian orphanage. She told me that she would mention something to the assistant superintendent and tell her that I wanted to talk to her the next time I was in Jefferson County for a meeting.

I happened to have a meeting in Jefferson County soon after we returned from Kansas City. I assumed that Dr. Donnie Hodges, assistant superintendent, would be too busy to stay after the meeting to talk to me about adoption. To my surprise, when Donnie saw me, she mentioned that she had spoken to Carolyn and she wanted to talk to me. After the meeting, she showed me pictures of her beautiful granddaughters and gave me a business card for an adoption agency in Atlanta. She answered all of my questions and told me that her son and daughter-in-law had a wonderful experience adopting with the help of that agency. She strongly encouraged me to contact them.

I subsequently contacted the adoption agency and met with them. I prayed to the Lord for guidance in making the right decision. After the agency answered all of my questions and provided all of the required paperwork, I decided to adopt a special needs orphan. They told me that if I would be very serious about the paperwork and complete all of the documents in the tedious multistep process in a timely manner, the adoption could possibly take only a year to complete. It was tedious, but I stayed focused and completed every required form as soon as possible and waited for a response from the Russian government.

I also knew that I needed to make some changes at work. My company was still my baby and was the way that I could financially support my new family. However, I had to make certain that I had the time I needed to be a good mother. I decided to move the company from Kennesaw (Atlanta area) to Warner Robins (middle Georgia), where I would be centrally located with the majority of my clients less than a two-hour drive from my office. This meant that I would no longer have to spend nights on the road staying at hotels. I could come home every night usually by 5 p.m. I also had to hire additional staff because I could no longer work sixteen-hour days, seven days per week.

In the fall of 2004, I received a call from my adoption agency to inform me that I had an appointment in Volgograd, Russia, in October to meet a child. It was an intimidating trip. I do not speak Russian and had never traveled outside of the country except for Mexico and Canada. The adoption agency was wonderful. They helped me make all of the travel arrangements and secure the services of a translator and bilingual driver when I was going to be in Volgograd and Moscow. They also found a Russian attorney for me who handled all aspects of the adoption.

In October 2004, I flew to Moscow and waited for my connecting flight to Volgograd. While waiting at the airport, I met a nice couple from Washington, DC, who were on their way to Siberia to adopt two biological sisters.

I arrived in Volgograd the next day. I immediately went to the government ministry office that handles adoptions. They gave me information regarding an eleven-month-old girl named Anastasia.

My translator's name was Kate. She went with me to the city orphanage in Volgograd. I did not know what to expect. My heart was racing and it was hard to contain my excitement. When I walked into the assigned room, there were approximately fifteen small toddlers and their caretakers. One of the women said, "There she is. There is your mama!" The most beautiful baby in the room jumped up and down in her arms and gave me a big smile and reached out to hug me.

I started crying. It was the first time that I met Kelsey. We bonded immediately. Kelsey was the most active and alert child in the room and was curious about everything. She had big bright blue eyes and a spunky spirit. The first English words that Kelsey heard were when I started to sing the "ABC" song and "Mary Had a Little Lamb." She looked at me as if it was the strangest thing she ever heard and smiled every time I started to sing the song again.

Figure 2 Kelsey at the orphanage in October 2004

The adoption agency had prepared me for what I saw at the orphanage. Although they cared about the children, the orphanage was very poor and could barely feed its children. Kelsey and the other children did not have any clothes or toys of their own. They had to share the same clothes and play with a shared box of old broken toys. They also did not wear diapers because the orphanage could not afford them.

The workers at the orphanage were not allowed to pick up the children and hug them. Instead they were ordered to always pick the child up from behind so the child couldn't see and hug them. They did this because the orphanage felt that if the children ever knew what it was like to be hugged, they would always want that attention. At night, all of the children were put into baby beds that were pushed against each other in a small room. The room would be locked, and no one would open the door until morning. The babies soon learned not to cry at night because no one was going to pay attention.

After I met Kelsey, the doctors at the orphanage wanted to talk to me. They sat me down in an office and wanted to make certain that I understood that Kelsey was a special needs baby. They said that their preliminary testing indicated that she probably had a serious heart condition. They also said that they could not guarantee me that she would ever walk or talk. I did not hesitate and told them that I had already fallen in love with her and wanted to adopt her. I told them that I would make certain she would get the best medical care possible.

*****

Two days later, on October 20, 2004, I went to the official government office and signed the initial papers. I had originally decided to name her Kelsey Elizabeth, but because I loved her birth name, I decided to name her Kelsey Anastasia. I was instructed to go back to the United States and wait for them to schedule a court date for the adoption.

The day I left to return to the United States was sad. They allowed me to stop by the orphanage on the way to the airport and say goodbye to Kelsey. They woke her up from her nap at 9:30 a.m. and she was still wiping sleep from her eyes when she

Figure 3 Kelsey at the orphanage in October 2004

saw me. She gave me a big hug and did not realize that she would not see me again for a few months. I cried on the way home on the plane and prayed to the Lord asking him to keep her alive and safe until I could return to Russia and bring her home.

I returned home and spent the next couple of months getting Kelsey's room ready and buying her Christmas and birthday presents and clothes. On December 27, 2004, I received a phone call from the adoption agency informing me that our adoption court date was scheduled for January 21, 2005, and because of the waiting time required for an adoption to become finalized, we would probably not be returning home to Bonaire until February 8.

It was a long wait to return to Russia. Each night, I prayed to the Lord asking him to keep Kelsey healthy and safe until I could see her again. On the day before I returned to Russia, January 15, 2005, I spent the day packing and buying last-minute items for the trip. I not only had to pack enough clothes for me to wear for a month, I had to pack clothes, diapers, bottles, baby formula, and everything Kelsey would need once I was allowed to take her from the orphanage. That night, I had dinner with Kelsey's godparents, Mike and Nancy Peacock.

On January 16, 2005, I left for the Atlanta airport at 6:30 a.m. When I was walking out the door of my house, I thought to myself, *This is the last time that I will be in my home. From now on, it will be our home.* My plane left Atlanta and arrived at JFK airport in New York at 1:30 p.m. During the several-hour layover, I spent time talking to my staff, friends, and relatives on my cell phone. I talked to Jodi Coren, the consultant on my staff who was going to be handling things at my office while I was gone. I had complete confidence in her. I called my friend and client, Carolyn Swint, who had been the person who made it possible for me to adopt Kelsey to thank her for making it possible. I also spoke to Kelsey's godparents again and promised that I would send them regular updates either by phone or email while I was in Russia.

As I was waiting to board the flight to Moscow, I wondered if Kelsey would remember me. During the flight, I sat next to a little

Russian boy who was traveling with a group of approximately twenty children. It was a long flight and when we arrived at the Moscow airport, my driver was waiting for me. He was irritated because someone had stolen the side mirrors from his car. It was snowing while he drove me to the Ukraine Hotel. He delivered a laptop computer, cell phone, and calling card that I could use while I was in Russia. While at the hotel, I bought some gifts for Kelsey, including an illustrated Russian fairytale book, a doll with a beautiful white costume, and a Matryoshka doll (Russian nesting doll).

That first day in Moscow seemed to last forever. I had to wait until the next morning (January 18, 2005) to leave for Volgograd. The reason was that they did not want me to fly because of the frequent blizzards in Volgograd in January. The adoption agency said that, often, their clients were in danger of missing their court dates because the planes were grounded due to hazardous weather con-

Figure 4 Moscow in October 2004

ditions. Instead, they recommended I take a twenty-hour train ride from Moscow to Volgograd.

The train station in Moscow looked like a scene from an old movie. I should have thought to take a picture, but I was so nervous and focused on seeing Kelsey again. I boarded the train at 2 p.m. in Moscow on January 18, 2005, and did not arrive in Volgograd until after 9:30 a.m. the next morning. I must admit it was scary getting on a train by myself where no one spoke English, knowing that I was headed straight through the heart of Russia and did not know what was waiting for me when we arrived at our destination. I sat in my compartment with the curtains open watching the Russian countryside. I had never seen so much snow. Much of the trip was through rural isolated parts of Russia that I would have never seen if I had flown. I had also never traveled by train before. It was an experience, and I could not wait to see Kelsey.

At 9:30 a.m. on January 19, 2005, my train arrived at the Volgograd train station. My translator and driver met me at the station and drove me to the Hotel Volgograd where I stayed while I was waiting for Kelsey. Later that morning, I met with my translator and my Russian attorney to go over the schedule for the next couple of days. I was so excited because I had an appointment at 12 noon at the orphanage to see Kelsey again.

I almost ran in the orphanage door at 12 noon. I became concerned when they would not let me enter Kelsey's room. They said the doctor wanted to talk to me first. My heart almost stopped. I was scared that they were going to tell me Kelsey had died while I was gone. The doctor asked me if I had ever had chicken pox. I told him that I had a very bad case of chicken pox when I was five. He said that was good because there was an outbreak of chicken pox at the orphanage and Kelsey might have it because she has red spots all over her body. Her illness might prevent us from leaving Russia as planned because she would not be able to pass the physical to leave the country if she had not fully recovered from chicken pox before we were scheduled to leave. This would mean we would stay in Russia longer than expected.

Figure 5 Kelsey at the orphanage in January 2005

After I spoke to the doctors, they let me see her. When I was there in October, they had been feeding her milk from a bottle that looked like a Coke bottle with a rubber tip on it. She was lactose intolerant and would throw up the milk as soon as she drank it. They had nothing else to feed her, so she was very thin (weighing less than fourteen pounds at fourteen months of age).

When I walked into the room, this time they were feeding her a bowl of soup and having her drink from a cup. When she saw me, she immediately smiled and reached out to me like she had known me all of her life. They allowed me to put her in a stroller and we walked around the orphanage. She opened her presents from her Christmas stocking that I had brought her. She liked the rabbit with chewable feet/hands and the multicolor chain links the best. She was not yet walking but could stand and bounce when I held her.

The next day, January 20, 2005, I took the subway and trolley with my translator, Kate, to see Kelsey at the orphanage. The adoption agency recommended that I use public transportation as much as possible while I was there on my second trip to save money. When we got to the orphanage, Kelsey had a fever from the chicken pox. She wanted me to hold her and she fell asleep as I was singing the "ABC" song to her. Her caregivers at the orphanage wished me good luck at the court proceedings that were going to take place the next day.

When we returned to the hotel that afternoon, I met with my translator and attorney. They prepared me for the court session. They explained the agenda format for the session and the type of information that needed to be included in my official verbal statement to the court. They even explained to me how to make the verbal statement by pausing periodically to allow my translator to repeat what I had just said in Russian to the judge. We practiced the timing so I could effectively communicate with the judge the next day.

I returned to my room and spent the rest of the evening preparing for the court session. I practiced making my official statement regarding why I wanted to adopt and reviewed the contents of my official home study and petition to the court. I only slept a couple of hours because I was so excited and nervous.

*****

On January 21, 2005, I met my translator in the hotel lobby, and we walked to the court building. I was very nervous, but she kept telling me that everything would be fine. At 9 a.m., we went to the judge's office on the fourth floor of the courthouse. During the proceeding, the electricity went out in the middle of my statement to the court, but the judge instructed me to keep talking with the lights out. At approximately 11 a.m., after a short recess, the judge read his order stating that he granted the petition and the adoption was approved. I was now officially Kelsey's mother.

Figure 6 Courthouse in Volgograd
in January 2005

I met with the translator and attorney later that morning to review the upcoming schedule. There is a waiting period for the adoption to become final. They will give me the official adoption papers on February 1, 2005, and I will pick up Kelsey from the orphanage and fly to Moscow on the evening of February 3, 2005 (if she has recovered from the chicken pox in time).

At noon, my translator and I took the subway to see Kelsey. On the way, we stopped at a children's store to buy diapers to take to the orphanage. It was cold and snowing. Kelsey's face had big red splotches on it. She looked like she did not feel well and was cranky because of the chicken pox. I held her hands, and she walked with me around the room and did not want to stop walking. The adoption agency had told me, when I first met with them, that these orphans realize when they finally have someone who loves them. They told me that her health would probably start to dramatically improve when she sensed that everything was going to be okay. It was amazing to see how Kelsey acted when I was there. The other thing the adoption agency told me was that my child was going to be very territorial about me and would not want the other children to get near me because I was *her* mother. That is exactly what Kelsey did. She did not want any other child to get near me because, for the first time in her life, she had somebody who loved her.

I met again with Kelsey's doctors. The doctor prepared a list of medicines that I could buy at the pharmacy to help them treat Kelsey's illness more aggressively. It was Friday and the doctors would be off all weekend, but if we brought the medicines on Monday, they would start giving her the medicines on Monday.

I returned to my hotel that afternoon and began calling people throughout the evening to tell them that the adoption had been approved. That evening, I spoke to my sisters, Jodi Coren (consultant on my staff who was running the office in my absence), Nancy Peacock (Kelsey's godmother), and several friends and clients from Georgia (Amy Rediger, Dianne Huff, Gloria Pylant, Brenda Lee, Debbie Connell, and Carolyn Swint).

They did not allow visitors at the orphanage on Saturdays and Sundays, so I could not see Kelsey again until Monday. On Saturday, January 22, 2005, my translator took me to see the Volgograd War Museum. Volgograd had been called Stalingrad during World War II. Stalingrad was the site of one of the deadliest battles of the war. She showed me the various exhibits and explained their significance. Everything was in Russian, so I would not have understood it if she had not been so helpful. We stopped by a pharmacy on the way back from the museum and I bought the medication on the list that Kelsey's doctor had given us.

On Monday, January 24, 2005, I returned to the orphanage with my translator, Kate. We delivered the medications to Kelsey's doctor and also the extra

Figure 7 Kelsey at the orphanage in January 2005

diapers for the other children. When Kelsey saw me, she hugged me and laid her head on my shoulder. The orphanage's social worker gave me a copy of the picture they took of Kelsey on the day she was admitted into the orphanage. On the way back from the orphanage, I bought a book regarding the history of Volgograd (in Russian and English) so Kelsey would have it as a future keepsake.

On January 25, 2005, I met Kate and a new translator, Tatiana, who would be helping me. When we arrived at the orphanage, the caregivers asked if I wanted to change Kelsey's diaper. Before I could finish changing her diaper, Kelsey kept trying to grab my neck so I would hold her. When I finally reached out to pick her up, she gave me a big hug and started laughing.

I had to stop wearing my jewelry (earrings and bracelets) because Kelsey liked playing with them (primarily trying to chew them). She also liked trying to chew my glasses.

On January 26, 2005, I visited the orphanage again. It was very cold. Kelsey was really starting to recognize me from across the room. She would do something and then look to see if I was watching her. Kelsey seemed to be feeling much better.

I had been warned by our American adoption agency that I had to be very careful during the waiting period when I was visiting the orphanage. I was allowed to visit Kelsey for a couple hours each day. During that time, I could sit on the floor in a corner of the room and watch Kelsey. However, I was not supposed to interact or take pictures of any of the other orphans. I was also supposed to be quiet and not complain about anything (so I would not accidentally offend the staff and jeopardize Kelsey's adoption).

Kelsey and the other children were obviously hungry and sick. I didn't realize just how small Kelsey was (fourteen pounds at fourteen months of age) because she was in the midrange compared to the other children. Some of the boys were much bigger and some other children were much smaller than Kelsey. They were all approximately—twelve to fourteen months old.

It was "snack" time. The worker reached into a cupboard and pulled out a loaf of bread. She started pulling off small pieces of bread to give to each of the toddlers. The bigger boys quickly ate their piece of bread and immediately started to pull the bread out of the smaller toddlers' hands and eat it. The smaller toddlers started screaming. They were starving and someone bigger than them had just taken the only food they were going to get to eat for several hours.

When the lady gave Kelsey her piece of bread, Kelsey immediately clenched it in her tiny fist and curled up into a fetal position with her body protecting the bread. The bigger boys approached her to take her bread, but she would not let them have it. They pushed, punched, and kicked her, but she would not let them get her food. They finally got tired of trying and moved on to some of the other small children.

As soon as they were on the other side of the room, Kelsey immediately put the bread in her mouth and ate it as fast as she could. I cried the entire time as I watched this brutal display of "survival of the fittest," but there was nothing I could do. If I would have tried to help her, they would have thrown me out of the orphanage and probably stopped her adoption. Kelsey's survival instincts and feisty personality kept her alive for the first fourteen months of her life when she had no one to protect her. No child should have to fight for food or even wonder if they are going to be able to eat today.

*****

On January 27, 2005, I was able to feed Kelsey and play with her on the playroom floor. The other children saw her sitting on my lap and wanted to sit by us. One little boy wanted me to hold and hug him. A music teacher came and played musical instruments and sang to the children. They enjoyed it.

When I left my hotel that evening to eat dinner, I saw an elderly man sitting in the fifth floor lobby by the elevator. He was moaning like he did not feel well and a couple of people were helping him. When I returned from dinner, I saw a dead body lying on the couch with a white sheet covering him. His feet were sticking out of the sheet. There were several hotel employees huddled around. When

I stopped momentarily, one them waved me down the hall toward my room.

Another situation that I witnessed in Volgograd sticks in the mind even after almost fifteen years. On my first trip to Volgograd, I had dinner with a group of Americans. It was later in the evening when we left the restaurant. When I was walking back to my hotel, I saw at least a dozen young unhealthy girls who looked like they were twelve to fifteen years old. They were standing on the sidewalks watching people pass by and stopping the men and trying to talk to them. I wondered what they were doing. One of the people next to me told me that they were prostitutes. She told me that many of these girls were orphans who, once they reached a certain age, were put out on the streets to fend for themselves. They had nowhere to go and no other way to support themselves. It was one of the saddest situations that I have ever seen.

Figure 8 Kelsey getting dressed to get her passport picture taken

On January 28, 2005, Tatiana and I used a car and driver to go the orphanage. After feeding and dressing Kelsey in a blue velvet sailor dress, we took her to a photography studio. The photographer took her passport photos. It was the first time she wore anything but orphanage rags. It was also the first time she had ever left the orphanage in a car. After returning to the orphanage, I played with Kelsey for another hour before I left for the day.

*****

January 29 and 30, 2005 (Saturday and Sunday). The orphanage did not allow visitors on Saturday and Sunday, so I spent the days walking and taking pictures for Kelsey's scrapbook. I was counting down the days until Kelsey and I could go home.

On Monday, January 31, 2005, we went to the orphanage. Kelsey cried when she saw me from across the room until I walked over to her and picked her up. She wanted me to hold her the entire time I was there. She started crying again when I started to leave and one of the caregivers picked her up and distracted her until I left the room. On the way to the hotel from the orphanage, I picked up Kelsey's passport and visa photos. Afterward, I met with my attorney to talk about the next day, and I bought our plane tickets to fly to Moscow on Thursday evening. I also called Delta Airlines and changed our flight reservations to New York to Sunday because Saturday's flight was full.

On Tuesday, February 1, 2005, I went to the courthouse and registry office to get the official court papers and birth certificate. After we had everything we needed, we went to the orphanage to visit with Kelsey. Again, she wanted me to hold her the entire time I was there. My translator talked to the doctor to obtain Kelsey's daily routine, meal plan, and medication list. After we left the orphanage, we bought thank-you presents for my attorney (a book), Kelsey's doctors (a box of chocolates), and the caregivers (lotion) at the orphanage. We also purchased Kelsey's medications, food, and a stroller.

On Wednesday, February 2, 2005, Tatiana (my translator) gave me Kelsey's daily routine and meal plan translated into English (from her doctor). I was really starting to get excited! Kelsey started crying again when she saw me because the ladies were changing her diaper and clothes, and I could not pick her up and hold her immediately. Her appetite was tremendous. She acted as if her lunch was the first meal she had in days. We took the gifts to the orphanage. The caregivers wrote a nice note in the Volgograd book that I bought for her.

The other children seemed jealous of the attention that I was giving Kelsey. She wanted to sit in my lap for most of the time I was there. Several of the other children wanted me to hold them and they started crying when they watched me hug Kelsey and hold her on my lap. There were approximately sixteen children, ages twelve to fourteen months in Kelsey's room. The majority of them were boys. I hoped that they got adopted soon by their new families.

Kelsey started crying when I had to leave. One of the caregivers had to hold her and play with her when I waved goodbye. That was going to be the last time I had to leave Kelsey in the orphanage because I was going to take her home the next day.

On the way back to the hotel, we stopped at a store to buy champagne and chocolates for the staff party the next day. We planned to buy the cakes on the way to the orphanage the next morning. I gave the translator the money to buy the special formula that the doctor had identified to feed Kelsey on the way home. She said that she knew the grocery store by her home had it.

Kate introduced me to a couple from New Jersey who was there on their first trip to find a child. Kate also brought me some of the documents that I was going to need for the American embassy in Moscow on Friday. I spent the remainder of the evening packing. I was so excited. This was my last night without Kelsey. Starting the next day, we would be a team.

On Thursday, February 3, I met with Tatiana and my attorney to obtain the remainder of the paperwork I would need for the American embassy in Moscow. Tatiana gave me the formula mix that the doctor recommended. One can contained a soy-based product and the other can contained a milk-based produce (to use if Kelsey refused the soy). My attorney took me to the government office to obtain Kelsey's Russian passport. After that, I met with the attorney and translator to review all of the official documents that I would need at the American embassy. They helped me organize the paperwork and understand why each document was important in the process. My attorney wished us well and said goodbye. My translator then helped me fax Kelsey's medical insurance adoption information to my insurance company in the United States requesting that they start to cover her immediately.

At 2:30 p.m. that afternoon, Tatiana and I went to the store to purchase two cakes (one for the caregivers and one for the medical staff) at the orphanage. At 3 p.m., we met Kate and the couple from New Jersey at the Manhattan restaurant for lunch. The New Jersey couple was going to be on the same flight to Moscow that evening and told me that they would help us if we needed anything on the flight.

Figure 9 Kelsey ready to get
dressed to leave orphanage

At 4:30 p.m., Tatiana and I left the hotel and traveled to the orphanage. They had just finished giving Kelsey a bath and she was wrapped in a towel. I gave them her new clothes and they put them on her. They posed for goodbye pictures with Kelsey. We gave them the cakes, chocolates, and champagne to thank them for taking such good care of Kelsey. The ladies were worried that the cute pink snowsuit that I had brought for Kelsey to wear was not warm enough. They gave me a pink woolen hat for Kelsey to keep her head warm. The ladies walked us to the front door and waved goodbye as we left. They asked me to send them copies of these pictures of Kelsey and other pictures as she grew up. One of them also asked me to make certain that Kelsey had dance lessons when she was older. I promised her that Kelsey would learn to dance. They were so happy for Kelsey and wished us well.

Driving to the airport, we could barely see the road and I was worried that the flight was going to be cancelled. At 5:30 p.m., we arrived at the old World War II—era airport. In the back of my mind, I realized that I was traveling with a medically fragile special needs child, and I was not certain how ill and fragile she was. We had heard that another special needs baby had just unexpectedly died at a

Moscow hotel while they were waiting to fly to the United States. I was on my own with her medically until we saw her new pediatrician in Macon the day after we arrived home. Tatiana and the driver helped me carry in all of our luggage and checked us in. We said goodbye and thanked them for everything they did while we were in Volgograd.

Lou and Marie Romano (the couple from New Jersey) arrived about 6 p.m. with Kate. Kate said goodbye to Kelsey. Lou and Marie were wonderful. They helped carry our carry-on bags with all of our official paperwork and Kelsey's things. They walked with us the entire time to make certain that I did not have difficulty carrying Kelsey to the transport bus. The bus transported us to the tarmac where an old plane sat on a runway. It was having mechanical difficulties and could not open the door on the side of the plane where passengers were supposed to board. Instead, they led us to the back of the plane and dropped some type of emergency collapsible stairs that looked like a ladder. I was expected to climb the "stairs" carrying a sick baby, a diaper bag, and my laptop. Thank goodness Marie took charge as I was looking up the "stairs" into the belly of the plane.

Figure 10 Leaving orphanage for the last time

Marie took my diaper bag and laptop and told Lou to go up the stairs behind me and, in case I started to fall, to grab the baby. We finally made it up the stairs and the old plane took off in terrible weather conditions.

Marie and Lou also offered to hold Kelsey if I had any problems during the flight, but their seats were several rows away from us. Kelsey and I sat down in our seat. We sat next to a nice Russian lady. Kelsey enjoyed the trip to Moscow. She drank water from a bottle and ate Cheerios one-by-one that I fed her. She seemed tired but did not let herself fall asleep because she might miss something. She also smiled and waved at the little boy sitting by us. Due to the bad weather conditions, it seemed like a miracle when we finally landed safely at the Moscow airport.

When we arrived in Moscow, Lou and Marie helped us carry everything to the baggage terminal. They waited with us until I found our driver. We said goodbye to Marie and Lou and sincerely thanked them for helping us. I don't know what we would have done without them. I had previously made arrangements for a bilingual driver to pick us up at the airport and drive us to the Ukraine Hotel. There were blizzard-like conditions in Moscow, and we were the only car on the road. I do not know how the driver could see the road. On the way to the hotel, we were stopped by a military-looking police jeep with two officers dressed in military gear, and they were carrying machine guns. They started yelling at us and our driver started yelling back—I thought we were all going to be shot. After they finished yelling at each other, the police officers walked away. I asked the driver what had happened, and he said, "I was driving too fast for the weather conditions." I have never been so glad to be an American!

We finally arrived at our hotel at 11 p.m. There was no baby bed in our room, so I had to call and complain. They finally brought one and Kelsey was able to get to sleep around 11:30 p.m. I stayed up late to unpack what we needed for Friday such as important papers for the American embassy, Kelsey's food, and our clothes.

On Friday, February 4, 2005, I woke up early and got ready. I also prepared Kelsey's breakfast (Gerber rice cereal and water). I watched Kelsey sleep and waited until 7 a.m. and woke her up. She was tired and didn't want to get up. Once I hugged

Figure 11 At Moscow hotel on February 3, 2005

her and showed her the food, she was hungry. I quickly fed and dressed her. We had to meet our driver downstairs in the lobby by 7:50 a.m.

Our driver drove us to the medical clinic. It was the first clinic that I had seen with guards patrolling the perimeter with machine guns (to prevent terrorist activity). Kelsey had an 8:30 a.m. appointment for her physical. It went well and they handed me a sealed envelope to give to the American embassy. Our driver took us to the American embassy where they made me leave our camera and cell phone at the front door. I took our paperwork to the appropriate window. While the lady reviewed the documentation, Kelsey and I went to the cashier window to pay for the visa. When we returned to the processing window, the lady had me sign a couple of forms and told me that the paperwork seemed to be in order. She gave us a form that said we needed to return at 2 p.m. for our appointment.

I took Kelsey back to the hotel for lunch and a nap, and we returned to the American embassy at 2 p.m. for the appointment.

Figure 12 At Moscow hotel on February 5, 2005

There were probably fifteen to twenty other American families there. The Russian children who were being adopted looked like they ranged in age from approximately six months to sixteen years old. The embassy official came out and explained the procedures to us and asked the parents to raise their right hand and swear that the information that we were sharing was accurate and we would abide by the rules and regulations. While he was talking, all of the other children were quiet, except for Kelsey. She was talking in baby talk. Everybody looked at us and smiled. When he said "Kelsey Norris," we went to the window. I sat Kelsey on the window ledge as I signed the official papers, and he handed me Kelsey's Russian passport with her American visa and three packets.

We returned to the hotel around 3:30 p.m. and Kelsey took a nap. When she awoke, I fed her dinner and we played. She went to bed around 8 p.m. and did not wake up until 9 a.m. the next day.

On Saturday, February 5, 2005, Kelsey did not wake up until 9 a.m. I fed her and dressed her in a very cute pale blue sweat suit with an angel on it. We played until 10:45 a.m. and then Kelsey took another nap. At 1 p.m., we went to the lobby and met our contact from the travel service. I returned the laptop and cell phone that I had rented from him. He introduced us to two American couples who were also working with our adoption agency who were on their first trip to Russia. One of the couples was from Acworth and was traveling with their three-year-old daughter, Nola. She said hello to Kelsey and Kelsey smiled at her. The family was going to be adopting a boy.

After meeting these families, we went to the gift store in the hotel lobby and bought some souvenirs for Kelsey. They included an ethnic costume with a headpiece and a traditional wooden children's toy. On the way back to our room, Kelsey continued to smile at everyone and several people spoke to her in Russian. She seemed to never meet a stranger. We then played until 7 p.m. (breaking only at 5 p.m. for dinner). I gave Kelsey a quick bath and she went to sleep immediately.

I stayed up to pack and get organized for our big trip the next day. I could not believe this day has finally arrived. If everything went smoothly, Kelsey would be an American citizen by 6 p.m. (New York time) when we landed in New York.

Figure 13 Hour 9 of a 10 hour flight to New York

On Sunday, February 6, 2005, Kelsey got up at 7:30 a.m. and had breakfast. I dressed her and finished packing the remaining items. At 9 a.m., our driver picked us up and we drove to the Moscow airport. We waited for another hour at the Friday's restaurant in the Moscow airport. It was the first time Kelsey had been inside of a restaurant, and she enjoyed sitting in a high chair eating Cheerios and drinking water.

At 11 a.m., we went through security and sat at our gate. I fed Kelsey another bottle. We boarded the plane around 12:30 p.m. and found our seat. Kelsey was good almost the entire trip. After approximately nine hours in the air, she started to get restless. At 3:25 p.m. (after ten hours in the air), we landed at JFK airport. At that time, Kelsey became an American citizen. We left the plane and walked to the immigration processing booths. Someone helped me carry our bag to the start of the American line. When we got to the booth, the man escorted us to the interview offices where they reviewed all of the forms in Kelsey's sealed visa packet. While I was busy signing forms, the lady yelled, "Oh my god, she has the red ink!" I looked over at Kelsey (who I was holding in my left arm) and she had grabbed the lady's Homeland Security red ink jar. Kelsey's hand was bright red and she already had gotten red ink on her face. I apologized to the lady and she quickly processed our remaining paperwork and had us escorted through immigration security. A nice couple (who were traveling with their little boy who had just been adopted from Russia) helped get our bags off the baggage carousel. The women pushed Kelsey's stroller as I pushed the baggage cart

Figure 14 At JFK Airport in New York

through the customs checkpoint and to the rechecking point for our bags (to check them to Atlanta).

After going to three different gates, we finally were sent to the right gate. We got on our plane and flew to Atlanta. At Atlanta, we got our luggage at baggage claim and paid a gentleman to take our bags to the car. We drove to Warner Robins with Kelsey sleeping most of the way home. We pulled into our garage at 11:30 p.m. I unloaded the car before waking Kelsey and taking her out of the car seat. Although she had been good the entire trip, she was very upset about being woken. I put her in her bed in my room and she went to sleep.

Figure 15 Celebrating Christmas on Feb 7, 2005

The next morning, on Monday, February 7, 2005, at 10 a.m., Kelsey woke up to her new home and her new life in Georgia. Her nose was red from being rubbed by her hand with red ink. We celebrated Christmas and she saw her new room for the first time. She also opened her birthday gifts. This was the beginning of the rest of her life. I was excited and proud to be part of it.

CHAPTER 3

Preschool Years

I had previously made an appointment with her new pediatrician in Macon before I left for Russia. On Tuesday, February 8, 2005, she had her first appointment with him. He examined her and said he did not detect any heart problems, although he was concerned with her small size and the need for her to use two hands when she picked up a Cheerio because she was too weak to hold it with one hand. He told me that the best thing I could do for Kelsey was to take her home and love her. He said we needed her to start growing and thriving and that would happen with love and the proper nutrition. He said that even though the Russian doctors said she had all of her current vaccinations, he wanted to start them all over again to ensure that she received them properly.

Figure 16 2nd Birthday Party in November 2005

On February 26, 2005, we had a wonderful welcome-home party for Kelsey at our house. We had over a hundred friends and clients come from throughout Georgia. It was a wonderful time. We celebrated Kelsey and the wonderful life she was going to have. It was a beautiful day full of friendship and love.

We were fortunate that I found a wonderful childcare facility, Meadowdale Learning Center, for Kelsey. She liked interacting with the other children and the staff and administration were top-notch. Kelsey had only been attending a few months when the director suggested to me that Kelsey might benefit from working with a private speech therapist who came every week to the center. I met with Natalie Keadle, the speech therapist, and she began working with Kelsey. Natalie made a tremendous difference in Kelsey's life and continually made helpful suggestions and provided me with the guidance I needed to make the right decisions regarding Kelsey's development.

Based upon Natalie's recommendation, I contacted the local school system's Child Find team, which screened Kelsey to determine if she needed preschool special education services. They determined that although she was developmentally delayed due to the year she spent in the Russian orphanage, she was on track and did not need preschool special education services other than speech therapy.

Figure 17 January 2007

When Kelsey was three years old, I talked to her pediatrician about what I could do to continue to help her developmentally. I told him that I wanted Kelsey to reach her full potential in life. I showed him a picture and article that someone had sent me about a little girl who looked like she could be Kelsey's twin. The girl in the picture had been diagnosed with having Rubenstein-Taybi syndrome (RTS). He said that he strongly doubted Kelsey had RTS because it is an extremely rare genetic disorder and most people have never even heard of it. In fact, it occurs in less than one in three hundred thousand births. People with this condition have small height (females are not usually taller than four eleven), moderate to severe learning disabilities, and an increased risk of developing cancer, leukemia, and lymphoma.

Children with RTS are more likely to be overweight, have a short attention span and poor motor and coordination skills. They are also likely to have scoliosis, digestive and urinary tract disorders, and heart problems.

Figure 18 At Sunday School in September 2007

He told me that if I insisted, he would give me a referral to the best specialist in the state who was the head of developmental pediatrics at Emory. Because the condition is so rare, the specialist sent us to the researchers at the University of Chicago to make the diagnosis. The reason was the University of Chicago is supposed to have the leading United States RTS researchers. When the experts at the University of Chicago made the diagnosis, they informed us that Kelsey's situation was extremely rare. Even though they had diagnosed other cases of RTS, Kelsey is the first person in the world who has been diagnosed with RTS with the specific genetic chromosomal defect that she has (i.e., they have never previously seen that specific genetic defect).

Figure 19 November 2008
Photo credit: Tamara Joiner

As you can imagine, the experts wanted to immediately enroll Kelsey in clinical research studies where she could have spent the rest of her life in hospitals and clinical labs. I told them no after they admitted that all of their research was not going to help Kelsey medically or developmentally. I made the decision for Kelsey to be able to have a happy, full, and meaningful life in the real world. I told them that, when Kelsey was older, if she made the decision to advocate for the developmentally disabled and for other children with medical conditions, I would support her 100 percent. I would be proud of her if she decided to address her disabilities in this manner.

I am thankful for the wonderful friends and support system we had while we were meeting with the specialist. I wanted them to attend the meetings with me to make certain that I asked the right questions and did not forget anything that was told to me. Kelsey's private speech therapist, Natalie Keadle, attended one of the meetings with us, and our friend, Gloria Pylant, who is a retired assistant school system superintendent, attended another meeting.

When we met to discuss her diagnosis, her specialist asked if he could ask me a personal question. When I said okay, he asked me if I regretted adopting Kelsey. I must have looked shocked and horrified, and he immediately apologized for asking the question. I said absolutely not. I knew she was a special needs adoption, and the doctors at the orphanage had told me that they could not promise me she would ever walk or talk. It was my responsibility to get her the medical care she needs and help her develop into her full potential. He said that the reason he asked the question was that many adoptive parents, who are told their new child has genetic/developmental disorders, have told him that if they had known it, they would not have adopted the child. I kept my mouth shut but, in my mind, I was thinking, *God knew what he was doing when he didn't give them biological children of their own.*

Figure 20 October 2011

Kelsey's specialist recommended that she be enrolled in a structured preschool program. He said her best chance of living a full life and reaching her maximum potential was for me to have high expectations for her. He said that she needed a strong academic focus with as many supports as possible. She had been attending a wonderful childcare facility with many enrichment opportunities, but this was not going to be the optimal solution for her.

I immediately researched available local preschool options and decided to enroll her in the Trinity Preschool program. It was a wonderful decision. The teacher was phenomenal. During our parent-teacher conferences, she told me that although Kelsey was developmentally delayed as compared to the other students, she was the politest student in the class. Her teacher said Kelsey always said please and thank you and was a joy to teach. I was also very grateful for the local school system who sent a speech therapist to Kelsey's preschool program to provide speech therapy services to help improve her communication skills.

When Kelsey entered Trinity Preschool at age three, she left Meadowdale Learning Center, which is where I had been relying on daily childcare for her. Trinity Preschool was just a half-day program ending before lunch each day. I had to hire a babysitter/nanny to pick her up from preschool each day and take care of her until I arrived home from work usually around 5:30 p.m. This worked well because she was also able to take Kelsey to her extracurricular activities in the afternoons before I arrived home from work.

CHAPTER 4

Extracurricular Activities

I wanted Kelsey to experience as much as possible. I also knew that children with Rubenstein-Taybi syndrome are more likely to be overweight and have poor motor and coordination skills. I began to look for extracurricular activities for Kelsey. Every day when I picked Kelsey up from Meadowdale Learning Center in Perry, I passed by a sign for KidsAmerica. The sign said that they provided gymnastics, dance, and cheer lessons. One day, I stopped by and talked to them. I subsequently enrolled Kelsey in gymnastics when she was two and dance when she was three.

KidsAmerica has been providing these services in middle Georgia since 1961. Mrs. Sally Stanley and her staff are some of the most wonderful people I have ever met. Their concept of youth development involves integrity and character development. They are interested in helping every child reach their full potential and, from the beginning, they have helped Kelsey grow and thrive. Kelsey was a little lamb in her first annual dance recital when she was three years old. That night she performed in front of several hundred people on a professional quality stage at the

Figure 21 At annual dance recital in May 2018

Warner Robins Civic Center. She has been performing in their annual dance recitals for the last twelve years.

I also saw a sign by my office for the Upward Sports Program at Second Baptist Church in Warner Robins when Kelsey was in preschool. Throughout the next several years, Kelsey participated in their soccer, tee-ball, softball, and cheerleading programs. She had a wonderful time in a safe, nurturing, and accepting environment where she met many friends and had a wonderful time interacting with the other children.

Figure 23 Summer 2009

Growing up, I had worked at the local public swimming pool in my hometown in Illinois and had taught Red Cross swimming lessons during high school and college. I recognized the dangers associated with child drownings and wanted Kelsey to learn to swim as soon as possible. However, her childcare facility would not let Kelsey swim in their pool with the other children because she had an occasional accident (usually due to her lactose intolerance). Kelsey was very disappointed and cried each day when the other children went outside for swimming lessons and pool playtime. I used my savings and had a pool installed in our backyard. I found Katie, an excellent Red Cross—certified water safety instructor, and paid her to give Kelsey swimming lessons. Kelsey learned to swim quickly and was soon diving and swimming underwater without fear. When she was old enough, I enrolled her in the Red Cross swimming lessons that the local recreation department was offering at their community pools.

Figure 22 Competing at a swim meet

She started with their most basic class and progressed through all of the classes they offered except for lifeguard training (because she was too young to take the lifeguard class).

When Kelsey was in early elementary school, she tried out for the Warner Robins Aquanauts Swim Team. On her second attempt, she made the team and has been swimming with them for the last seven years. I cannot say enough positive things about this organization. Coach Wes Hamborg and his staff are terrific and have been tremendous role models and mentors for Kelsey. The water is her home and she could spend all day in the pool if I let her. Swimming is such a wonderful sport. All children should have access to a pool and a swimming program.

I know many families with developmentally disabled children struggle every summer trying to find appropriate summer camp opportunities. We have never had that problem. Natalie, our private speech therapist, strongly recommended that I enroll Kelsey in the National STEM Academy summer camps conducted by the Warner Robins Museum of Aviation. The camps focus on a variety of topics such as engineering, space and rocketry, oceanography, and robotics. Kelsey has been attending their hands-on educational and enrichment camps since she was four years old with general education students. The staff are experienced educators who have a knack for making learning fun. We are fortunate to have such a high-quality summer learning opportunity in middle Georgia.

When Kelsey was in middle school, she asked me if she could

Figure 24 At a horse show in August 2018

take horse-riding lessons. She loves spending one afternoon each week riding her instructor's horse. Kelsey has an excellent instructor, Tiffany Turner, who is patient and has taught Kelsey many riding skills during the past year. Riding Charlie has a calming effect on Kelsey, and the horse just seems to care about her. Kelsey seems to be especially drawn to animals. She understands them and they seem to understand her.

CHAPTER 5

Experience in the General Education Environment

Nothing could have prepared us for the odyssey that began when Kelsey entered the local public school system. I have worked for public school systems throughout Georgia for the last twenty-five years. Some of my best friends are school administrators and teachers. I think that teaching is one of the most noble and important professions that exist. A good teacher can make a tremendous positive difference in a child's life.

We eagerly anticipated Kelsey starting school at the local elementary school. She started school in the prekindergarten program in August 2008 and loved it. Her teacher and paraprofessional were wonderful, kind, and patient individuals who were experienced educators. Kelsey thrived in that loving and nurturing environment. When it came time to review the results of the annual standardized testing at the end of prekindergarten, I was nervous about what her teacher was going to tell me. I was

Figure 25 First day of Pre-Kindergarten in August 2008

39

afraid that Kelsey was behind academically and wanted to do everything possible to help her progress. Her teacher told me that Kelsey tested "in the middle of the pack" as compared to her prekindergarten classmates. She was tiny (weighing less than thirty pounds) and obviously was still trying to catch up developmentally with children her age due to the year she spent at the Russian orphanage prior to her adoption. However, academically she was not behind the class.

Her transition into kindergarten, however, was not a smooth one. On the first day of class, her teacher called me and told me that she was not happy with Kelsey. Apparently, on the first day of class, the teacher was at the front of the room explaining the Germanic significance of the words *Kinder* and *garten.* During this lecture, Kelsey apparently yawned and laid on the floor pretending to sleep (and snore). Her classmates thought she was funny and laughed. Her teacher was highly offended and bewildered at the thought of a five-year-old child not being mature enough to understand her historical lecture on the meaning of the word *kindergarten.* I knew immediately that Kelsey was probably in the wrong classroom.

Throughout the year, the teacher made it clear that she did not like teaching Kelsey and, at one point, I met with the school principal and her. I told her that I realized she did not like teaching a student who was developmentally behind (Kelsey was a special education student receiving speech therapy). I told them that I wanted to hire a tutor and work with her myself. The principal asked me what I wanted from the teacher. I simply said to the teacher, "Kelsey loves you. Please do not break her heart or her spirit." Her teacher replied, "I know it must be hard to hear for the first time that your princess isn't perfect." I decided to ignore her remark and politely smiled at her (although it was very difficult to maintain my composure).

While I was walking out of his office, the principal stopped me and made some casual comments such as "Kelsey is so much smaller than the other children. Her eyes have an unusual shape. We wouldn't be surprised if she has fetal alcohol syndrome. You will never know for certain because she is from a foreign orphanage." I was taken aback by the unexpected commentary but decided to take a big deep breath and ignore the comment. While I was walking to my car, I thought to myself that these people were clueless. It disappointed me to realize how little they actually knew or understood about their own students.

The kindergarten year was difficult; however, we got through it with Kelsey receiving tutoring assistance from an excellent tutor. Kelsey and I read together every night and worked on everything her teacher and her tutor recommended. She also had a wonderful paraprofessional, Angela Livingston, in her kindergarten classroom who looked out for Kelsey and kept her safe.

During her kindergarten year, the school sent home a form that I was told was mandatory for me to complete. It asked questions regarding where Kelsey was born, what her native language was, etc. I had never seen anything like this before and I contacted her teacher and told her that I was confused about some of the questions and asked why I had to complete and return it. The school knew Kelsey was born in Russia and was adopted when she was fourteen months old. She never learned to speak, read, or write in Russian. English is the only language she knows. The teacher told me not to worry about it and to complete the form and send it back to school. She said that if I had made any mistakes/typos on the form, I would have an opportunity to correct them. I followed her instructions and completed and returned the form.

Figure 26
Kindergarten
school picture in
August 2009

Needless to say, I was shocked when I received an official letter from the school system informing me that Kelsey had been put into the English as a Second Language (ESOL) program and there was a possibility that Kelsey was going to be removed from her elementary school and sent to a school on the other side of the county that served ESOL students. I immediately called the school system's ESOL contact number. The person I spoke with told me that because I checked a specific box on the official form, it was now mandatory to place Kelsey in the ESOL program. I told her that I did not fully understand how to correctly complete the form, and it was a typo because English is the only language Kelsey knows. She told me that, unfortunately, according to federal law, I was not allowed to change my response on the form and that Kelsey would be a mandatory participant in the ESOL program until she tested out of it or graduated. I told them that Kelsey would not be attending the ESOL school because she did not speak the same language of any of the other students that would be there. After they realized how angry I was, they backed down and did not make Kelsey leave her elementary school.

Every year since then, they tested Kelsey to determine how fluent she was in reading, writing, and speaking English. Each year, she did not reach the threshold to exit the program. Each year, I pointed out to them that the reason she did not reach the threshold was because she has developmental disabilities. It was not because English was her second language. Each year, they said they agreed with me but there was nothing the school system could do. This ridiculous cycle continued until Kelsey was transitioning from eighth grade into high school. The school system suddenly officially decided that the reason Kelsey had not tested out of the ESOL Program for the past eight years was because she had developmental disabilities. At that point, they finally allowed her to leave the ESOL Program.

This is particularly disappointing to me because I know there are hundreds of thousands of ESOL students in this state who need a great deal of resources and assistance in order to be successful in school. The staff time and resources that were used to test and monitor Kelsey were a waste of taxpayer funding. However, the most disappointing aspect of this situation is the thought that parents (most of whom have limited English proficiency) would get no assistance in completing this form in English and receive no flexibility in correcting any errors. I am just one example of a parent who received no assistance or guidance in completing this form and my child had to live with the consequences of me checking one box incorrectly for over eight years.

In May 2010, during the last month of her kindergarten year, I received one of the biggest surprises of my life. Kelsey's babysitter/nanny had been working for us for over two years. She helped me take Kelsey to school and pick her up each day. She also was responsible for caring for Kelsey after school and taking her to her extracurricular activities until I arrived home from work each day. It was a financial hardship for me to hire her, but I needed help taking care of Kelsey after school. I thought I had found a reliable caring person to fill the position. I gave her a competitive salary and a full benefits package including health insurance. Throughout the years, the nanny had asked me several times if she could borrow money because of needing to pay light bills, rent, medical bills, etc. Each time, I had personally loaned her money because it always sounded like an emergency and she had been good to Kelsey. Sometimes she paid me back and sometimes she did not. I never questioned her about this because we thought she was a wonderful, kind, and caring person who loved my daughter.

In May 2010, I noticed that my company's bank account was unexpectedly low. I couldn't figure out why because I knew we had sufficient funds in the account to make payroll and meet our expenses. I immediately went online and reviewed my bank records, including copies of checks that had cleared the bank. I was horrified to discover that someone had stolen blank checks from the secure place that I was storing them at home and written several checks made out to our nanny and signed my name. These checks totaled over six thousand dollars. The day I found the checks, the nanny was working in the kitchen with Kelsey. I asked Kelsey to go outside in the backyard to play on the swing set. I then asked the nanny about the checks. At first, she said she didn't know what I was talking about and someone was lying to me about her. Then I showed her copies of the canceled checks with her name on them. When she realized that I had proof of what she had done, she said that it was no big deal because it wasn't that much money. I told her that it was a large amount of money that I did not have. I told her that I had trusted her and was shocked and disappointed. I told her that she was terminated effective immediately and she needed to leave our house. After she left, I called the locksmith and had all of the locks in the house changed. I then called the police and made a police report. Several days later, they arrested her. When she was released on bail, she was told not to have any contact with either Kelsey or me. The nanny made some statements to people that she wanted to see "her baby" and, if I would not let her come to the house, she would go to school and talk to Kelsey.

I do not like sharing my personal business with strangers, but I felt it was necessary, for Kelsey' safety, to drive to the school and talk to her principal. I told him what had happened and asked that they remove the nanny's name from the list of people authorized to pick Kelsey up from school. I also told him that the nanny was not allowed to come to school to talk to Kelsey. I asked him that, if the nanny showed up at school, to immediately call law enforcement and then call me on my cell phone. He said that the school would do that.

I was stunned when the principal told me that the nanny had been behaving inappropriately at school for the past year. I asked him to explain to me what he was talking about. The nanny had asked me at the beginning of the year if she could volunteer at school during the day while I was paying her. She said that the school staff had suggested it to her while she was picking up Kelsey one day. I said that I didn't mind her volunteering as long as that is what the school wanted. I reminded her that I knew all school volunteers had to go through a background check process and she needed to follow all of their rules. I was impressed that she cared enough about my daughter to want to help.

The principal told me that while the nanny was at the school "volunteering" that year, she had been walking the halls asking teachers and other staff members to loan her money. Apparently, the principal and some of the other staff members had actually loaned her money. Furthermore, at least one staff member (Kelsey's kindergarten teacher) was profiting financially from the nanny by loaning her money with "interest." At some point during the school year, the principal said he had to have a staff meeting to tell his staff not to loan her any additional money. I was appalled. I asked him why he didn't immediately contact me when he discovered the nanny was asking people for money while she was volunteering at the school (and being paid by me). He didn't have an answer for me.

I became even more concerned when people suddenly started contacting me when they heard the nanny had been fired. Apparently, the nanny had been approaching staff members and other parents at Kelsey's extracurricular activities (e.g., dance, gymnastics, cheerleading, tee-ball, etc.) for money. While I thought the nanny and Kelsey were home each afternoon safely playing in the backyard, the nanny had been driving all over the county with Kelsey in the back seat of her car, asking people to loan her money and trying to avoid others who wanted to be paid back. My daughter's life could have been endangered during that year. If the school had simply notified me of this problem when it first started to happen at school, I would have talked to the nanny and terminated her employment with us. She would not have been able to take over six thousand dollars from my company and, perhaps, endanger my daughter's life. I have no reason to believe that Kelsey was hurt in any way, but she could have been. The nanny was eventually convicted and we have never seen her again. The principal was promoted, at the end of the school year, to assistant superintendent.

The other issue that concerned me a great deal about kindergarten was how the kindergarten teacher was assessing Kelsey. I noticed when Kelsey received her first report card that the teacher had indicated Kelsey was not meeting standards such as not knowing the days of the week or months of the year. Kelsey learned those in preschool and could recite them forward and backward. I asked the teacher what was the problem and she said that Kelsey would not meet those standards until she could spell all of them. That is just one example. I contacted friends who were kindergarten teachers in other school systems to ask them what I didn't understand about these standards. They told me that, although they couldn't comment on what was happening in Kelsey's classroom, it sounded as if Kelsey was meeting the standard examples I was describing to them. They suggested that I go online and visit the Georgia Department of Education website and review the standards myself. I printed a copy of the Georgia kindergarten standards and put it in a three-ring notebook. I took the notebook when I subsequently met with Kelsey's principal. I gave him specific examples of the standards that Kelsey had been meeting for over a year and asked if I was misinterpreting the standards. He said that I was correct and he would talk to Kelsey's kindergarten teacher and get back to me. At our subsequent meeting, he gave me a vague explanation about how Kelsey's teacher had higher standards than the state and that was a good thing. I told him that I still did not understand why Kelsey would be held to higher standards than the students in the other kindergarten classrooms in the state.

Throughout the entire school year, I felt that I did not understand the entire situation. I felt that there was something else that Kelsey and I were not doing to cause the number of standards she was meeting on her report card to be artificially low. When the situation with the nanny was exposed suddenly at the end of the school year, it all made sense. I realized that there was the strong possibility that Kelsey was never going to get credit for the standards she was meeting while the nanny still owed the kindergarten teacher money. This was a rude awakening for me as a parent. Until that year, I never even imagined that this situation would be allowed to occur in a public school system in Georgia.

When it came time for first grade, Kelsey was super excited. I took her to get her hair cut and buy a new pair of school shoes. We attended open house and met her first grade teacher. She seemed very disorganized, but I just assumed that it was because open house was a very busy day and she was tired. When we were walking down the hallway to leave the building, we ran into another parent whom we knew. We said hello and she asked who Kelsey's first grade teacher was. When I told her, she looked horrified and asked me if I realized that the first grade teacher was best friends with her old kindergarten teacher. I should have listened when she told me to go straight to the new principal's office and request that Kelsey be moved to another first grade classroom. I naively assumed that everyone was a professional and the students were their number one priority.

Kelsey was eager to start the school year and meet new friends when school started on August 9, 2010. I sent Kelsey to school on August 9 and assumed she was going to have a great time in a regular first grade classroom. When she returned home from school that first day, she seemed quiet and didn't have much to say. I asked Kelsey how she got the bruises on her arms and legs and she said she did not remember. (In retrospect, I think she was too embarrassed to tell me about the bullying.) I thought that it might take a few days to get used to a new routine and wasn't worried at that point.

On August 16 (eight days after school had started), I received a note from her first grade teacher asking me if we could have an "informal meeting to talk about how we could work together to make this a successful year for Kelsey" on August 17. I immediately called her first grade teacher and asked if anything was wrong and the teacher stated, "Absolutely not." She said that the meeting was just an informal opportunity to get to know each other better.

On August 17, I arrived at school and went to the classroom where the meeting was scheduled to take place. The Early Intervention Program (EIP) reading and math teachers were waiting for me. Her first grade teacher arrived late to the meeting after the EIP teachers informed me that Kelsey has been enrolled in the first grade Early Intervention classroom since the first day of school (August 9, 2010). She had never been assigned to a regular first grade classroom and no one had told me. No one knew why I had not been informed earlier. They said the reason for this was that Kelsey was only reading on the "A" reading level and had very low math skills. I mentioned to the group that Kelsey's previous tests had indicated that Kelsey had average or above average math skills, and she had been reading at the "C" level during the summer. They explained to me that the tests they do are more thorough and accurate. They also explained that sometimes students regress during the summer.

While I was very concerned regarding being invited to a meeting under false pretenses, I was impressed with the professionalism displayed by the EIP teachers and agreed to work with them in any manner possible. I was told that, although her first grade teacher would actually be considered her teacher, the EIP teachers would visit the classroom daily and work with Kelsey and the other students. When I returned home that evening, I found a form letter in Kelsey's backpack informing me, in writing (dated August 16, 2010), that Kelsey had been placed in the EIP program.

On September 28, 2010, the first grade teacher sent a note home in Kelsey's agenda requesting that I work with Kelsey to practice writing stories. After reading this instruction in Kelsey's agenda, I immediately started working with Kelsey to write short stories every evening. On September 28, I also agreed for the school system's occupational therapist to conduct an assessment on Kelsey to determine if she could benefit from occupational therapy services.

On October 6, 2010, I received a Tier 2 notification letter (dated September 28) from the school's guidance counselor stating that Kelsey had been referred to the team due to "academic difficulties." On October 14, 2010, I called the school office and spoke to one of the assistant principals to share my concerns regarding the first grade teacher's lack of sensitivity regarding Kelsey's developmental delays. The assistant principal said that she would address these issues with the teacher.

On October 15, 2010, we had Kelsey's first student support team meeting. The participants included the assistant principal, guidance counselor, first grade teacher, and me. The first grade teacher began the meeting with announcing that Kelsey has serious academic problems. When asked to give an example, she showed a paper where Kelsey had started to write off the right-hand side of the page with the letters on top of each other. She said that this was a good example of the best Kelsey can do regarding writing.

I asked the first grade teacher why she had not also brought copies of the fourteen short stories that Kelsey has written at home since September 28 (when the teacher had first requested me to work with Kelsey at home writing). The teacher's face turned red and she stated that she had not seen the stories. I said that, in fact, she had seen them because they were written in Kelsey's homework notebook and the teacher had written comments on them after she had reviewed them. I, subsequently, shared copies of the fourteen short stories with the student support team meeting participants. They were surprised by the existence of the short stories and listened to me as I shared tips and techniques regarding how I work with Kelsey to write stories. The assistant principal and the guidance counselor began to also give the teacher advice on how to work with Kelsey. The teacher became irritated and announced that she needed to leave the meeting to be with her other students.

The teacher left the room and returned five minutes later stating that she had made arrangements regarding her other students. I then pulled my laptop from my briefcase and showed the meeting participants a video of Kelsey identifying ninety-three of her one hundred sight words. Those were the words that Kelsey needed to correctly identify by the end of first grade in May 2011. The assistant principal and guidance counselor complimented Kelsey on this accomplishment so early in the academic year. I also had a video of Kelsey reading an "E" level book, but, in the interest of time, did not show it. The meeting was adjourned with the assistant principal and the guidance counselor expressing their pleasure with Kelsey's academic progress to date.

On October 21, 2010, I experienced the most bizarre parent-teacher conference that I could have ever imagined. The meeting was scheduled to last twenty minutes and it actually lasted one hour and fifteen minutes. The teacher was disorganized and spent a great deal of time during the meeting looking for Kelsey's homework and other papers to show me. She was defensive regarding why I could work with Kelsey and she could not. She told me that "If Kelsey is supposedly reading at an E level, she should be able to write at an E level." She also said that "Kelsey is deliberately defying me—she is playing me." I replied that, although I am not an educator or an occupational therapist, I have been told that if a child needs occupational therapy services, the child may be able to read much better than he/she can write due to weak fine motor skills.

During the parent meeting, the teacher answered her cell phone. The caller was another teacher's daughter from Colorado who was applying for a special education teaching position at one of the other elementary schools in the system. Kelsey's teacher continued to talk to her while I was sitting in the room expecting a parent-teacher conference. I could hear the other person talking because the phone was loud. Kelsey's teacher continued to chat with the phone caller. The caller asked the teacher to find her mother (another teacher at Kelsey's school) and that she needed help trying to influence a member of the interview committee into deciding to hire her. Kelsey's teacher agreed to help and finally ended the phone call. She explained to me how important the phone call was and that she was excited to know that her good friend's daughter was possibly going to work for the school system.

I was extremely concerned regarding Kelsey's teacher's lack of interest in the parent-teacher conference and mentioned to her that it was getting late and I needed to leave (after sitting in the classroom for one hour and fifteen minutes). I asked the teacher if I could receive a copy of Kelsey's report card (that was the reason why I attended the meeting). Her teacher gave me a copy of the report card. I looked at the card and politely asked why Kelsey had so many 1's on issues such as writing and reading. The teacher told me that she was required to complete and submit the report card several weeks prior to the end of the grading period. She stated that if she was completing it now, Kelsey's scores would more accurately reflect her academic status. She ended the meeting by stating she "was not worried about Kelsey academically."

November 1, 2010, was the first day of school after Halloween. Kelsey ate an enormous amount of candy on Halloween and didn't feel well when she went to school on November 1. Apparently, her teacher told her to leave the classroom and go sit in the special education classroom. Kelsey left the classroom, as instructed, and ran to the special education classroom. She got into trouble for running. When I asked Kelsey why she ran, Kelsey told me "that classroom is safe and they will not let anyone hurt me." I later found out that after Kelsey left the first grade classroom, her first grade teacher asked her old kindergarten teacher to come to the classroom. The kindergarten teacher just coincidentally happens to be the mother of the phone caller from Colorado who wanted assistance securing a position with the school system. She is also the same teacher who loaned Kelsey's nanny money with "interest" while Kelsey was in kindergarten. The kindergarten teacher asked Kelsey's classmates to "raise your hand if Kelsey has hit them today." I called Kelsey's first grade teacher that evening to ask why another teacher would come into her classroom and single out Kelsey in front of her classmates. Her teacher replied, "Kelsey was not present when the other teacher talked about her with the other students." I expressed my concern regarding this unprofessional behavior and told her that I feared Kelsey's rights had been violated and that the other teacher "planted the seed" in the minds of the other students and parents that Kelsey is a problem.

On November 4, 2010, we met at the school for Kelsey's IEP (Individualized Education Plan) meeting to modify her existing IEP plan to include occupational therapy. The meeting included a special education teacher, speech therapist, occupational therapist, guidance counselor, assistant principal, and me. We reviewed the results of the recent occupational therapy evaluation. We determined that Kelsey needed to receive occupational therapy services for thirty minutes each week. Occupational therapy services began the following week. We discussed some additional services/equipment that could be provided such as items that can be chewed, weighted backpack, stress balls, etc. After I returned home from the IEP meeting on November 4, 2010, I heard a voice mail message from her teacher requesting that I return to the school immediately because there is a problem in the classroom. I immediately returned to the school and went to Kelsey's classroom. When I arrived, all of the students (including Kelsey) were sitting on the floor participating in some type of lesson. Kelsey's teacher came to the classroom door and informed me that the situation had been handled. She told me that she had to ask Kelsey more than once to spit out her gum into the wastepaper basket. (Note: The teacher previously gave Kelsey the gum and allowed her to chew it to avoid having Kelsey chew other objects.)

Her teacher instructed Kelsey to come out into the hallway so I could discipline Kelsey for her teacher having to ask her more than once to spit out the gum. I told Kelsey that I expected her to listen to her teacher and I left the school for the second time that day.

On November 5, 2010, I called the assistant principal to express concerns regarding the parent-teacher conference incident with the other teacher talking to the class about Kelsey, bullying, and other related issues. The new principal subsequently called me and invited me to meet with him. I immediately drove to the school and met with the principal, assistant principal, and guidance counselor. I described the current situation, including sharing that Kelsey was now afraid to go to school. She cried every morning and said that her teacher didn't like her and the other children made fun of her when the teacher yelled at her. I told them that Kelsey was being bullied and I was afraid that the teacher was doing the majority of the bullying. The principal listened to my concerns and said that he would immediately talk to the first grade teacher and investigate my concerns. This included him personally monitoring the first grade classroom.

Starting in November, the principal and other administrators took turns monitoring the first grade classroom. The principal sub-sequently informed me that they had found that Kelsey was being unfairly/inappropriately singled out by her first grade teacher. He told me that they were going to work with her first grade teacher and provide additional educational opportunities regarding classroom management and interacting with students and parents. He said that while the first grade teacher did not believe she was doing these things, she was willing to change and become more sensitive to how she was treating Kelsey. He also informed me that the first grade teacher was having difficulty with several other students besides Kelsey.

Although I was very thankful that my concerns were addressed, I was scared to death for Kelsey because I suspected that the first grade teacher and her friends were going to retaliate by making Kelsey's academic experience a living hell. Unfortunately, I was cor-rect. On November 17, 2010, Kelsey received a disciplinary referral for disrespecting a teacher and disobeying her when instructed to go to her classroom. Instead, Kelsey ran into the bathroom. When I asked Kelsey why she had not listened to the teacher and gone to the classroom as instructed, Kelsey said that she "had to go potty really bad." I explained to Kelsey that teachers do not like to be disrespected and that, even if she has an accident in her pants, it would be better to have the accident than to get in trouble and be sent to ISS. I told Kelsey that she would not be in trouble if she has an accident at school, as long as the teacher is satisfied with her behavior.

On December 1, 2010, we had Kelsey's second student support team meeting. Prior to the meeting, I contacted the guidance counselor to verify the meeting's time and location. I also asked her who would be present at the meeting. She told me that the participants would be the same as the previous meeting (guidance counselor, first grade teacher, and assistant principal) with the addition of the EIP reading teacher who would share information regarding Kelsey's reading progress.

When I arrived for the student support team meeting on December 1, 2010, there was a room full of people including the: principal, assistant principal, guidance counselor, EIP math teacher, and at least four first grade teachers. I must admit that I was very intimidated. In retrospect, I can't image how the typical parent would have reacted to that scenario. I have a master's degree and have spent my entire career (over twenty-five years) making presentations and meeting with school board members, administrators, and teachers. However, I had never seen anything like this. Research documents that many parents may be individuals who have not graduated from high school and may have had a bad educational experience themselves. I can't imagine having a struggling single mother, who is already scared to be in the school environment, walk into a room with such an unexpectedly hostile environment.

I took a big deep breath and reminded myself that I was there to positively advocate for my daughter and that I should expect everyone present to handle themselves in a professional manner. I started the meeting by giving a copy of Kelsey's new self-published book (containing a compilation of fifty short stories written between September 28 to November 27, 2010) to the principal. I announced that everyone in the room would receive a copy of the book as a Christmas present from Kelsey. When I started to review it with the participants, all of the other teachers (except her first grade teacher) stood up in unison and walked out of the room while I was in mid-sentence. (I am assuming it was a way to intimidate me and formally show their lack of respect for me as a parent.) Ten minutes later, her first grade teacher stood up and said that "If I'm not needed, I need to get back to my classroom." While she was leaving the room, she muttered, "I guess you will let me know what strategies I am supposed to work on with Kelsey."

After her first grade teacher left the room, I continued to meet for at least another thirty minutes with the principal, assistant principal, and guidance counselor. They agreed that Kelsey was continuing to make good academic progress. I expressed my concerns that the occupational therapy follow-up steps identified during the recent IEP meeting had not yet occurred. The assistant principal and guidance counselor said that they shared my concerns and that they were in the process of following up with the occupational therapy department.

On December 4, 2010, Kelsey and I held our annual Christmas party at our home (in our backyard) with Santa and approximately 150 other individuals. Kelsey invited her entire first grade class and also gave an invitation to her teacher. Her teacher attended the party and at the end of the party (after all other school staff had left) walked into the kitchen area of our home. I was talking to several other guests in the room. Her teacher approached me and announced that Kelsey has displayed some odd behavior earlier in the week while she was in transit to the cafeteria (e.g., Kelsey was running to the cafeteria despite being told to slow down). She continued to make negative comments regarding Kelsey. The three other individuals in the room became very uncomfortable and several other guests started to enter the room but turned away after hearing the tone of the teacher's voice and the content of her remarks. After the teacher left, I was complimented on my ability to remain calm and I was told that I "handled the situation with class and avoided open conflict" by listening quietly and thanking the teacher for attending the party. The witnesses stated that they felt the teacher's comments were strange, unprofessional, and inappropriate to be shared outside of the school building in front of strangers. One witness said, "Kelsey doesn't stand a chance in that classroom." I was strongly encouraged to meet with the principal on the following Monday morning and immediately remove Kelsey from the classroom. Other parents/guests who overheard the teacher's remarks approached me and expressed support and concern for Kelsey.

In December 2010, Kelsey was invited by various civic groups, Even Start Family Literacy Programs, preschool programs, daycare early learning centers, and senior citizens' centers to serve as a featured speaker/program. They wanted me to introduce her by mentioning some of the key human interest facts included in her book. Then they wanted Kelsey to share a short story from her own book and subsequently read a second grade level reading book. I told these groups that I had to coordinate their meeting schedules with Kelsey's school schedule because I would not allow her to miss school.

On the morning of December 13, 2010, I distributed copies of Kelsey's self-published book (we made Xerox copies) to all of the school administrators, guidance counselor, speech therapist, and previous/current teachers and paraprofessionals. I immediately started to receive positive feedback and expressions of support and encouragement for Kelsey.

Later in the day on December 13, 2010, Kelsey received a disciplinary referral and was sent to ISS (in school suspension) on December 14. She received the referral because she colored on another child's desk, crawled on the floor, hit students, threw blunt-edge scissors, threw papers off of the rocking chair, and soiled herself. Kelsey had severe diarrhea during the previous weekend. On December 13, it had stopped for twelve hours, so I sent her to school (this was my mistake). At 9 a.m., Kelsey had another diarrhea accident. She was sent to the medical technician, and Kelsey had to change herself into new clothes and was sent back to the classroom. Due to the severity of the diarrhea, Kelsey was unable to adequately clean herself and was embarrassed to ask anyone for help. Therefore, she had to sit all day in her own drying feces. As the day progressed, she became increasingly irritable with severe stomach cramps, but due to her developmentally delayed communication skills, she was unable to express her discomfort.

At 2:45 p.m., she had another severe episode of diarrhea and there was no way to clean her adequately. They called us to pick her up from school. After Kelsey arrived home, I removed her clothes to give her a bath. At the time, I discovered a rash, skin discoloration, and blisters resulting from having dried feces on her body for an extended period of time. I subsequently called the pediatrician's office and requested advice. The nurse told me to monitor Kelsey throughout the night, and if she had any further incidents of diarrhea, to keep her home from school the next day.

Kelsey did not have another accident that evening and was sent to school on December 14 to spend the day in ISS. I called the school's medical technician and asked why Kelsey was not sent home at 9 a.m. the previous day when she had her first severe diarrhea episode at school. That would have prevented her suffering all day and behaving in a manner that caused her to be sent to ISS. She apologized and said that she had helped Kelsey clean herself and did not realize that Kelsey had diarrhea. She told me that if she had known about the diarrhea, she would have sent her home immediately. I accepted her apology and asked her to please monitor Kelsey closely during the day. I called the medical technician again later in the day to check on Kelsey's health status and was informed that Kelsey was fine. However, I subsequently discovered, from another individual, that Kelsey fell asleep several times during ISS and when she was waiting to be picked up from school. Kelsey attended school the remainder of the week even though it was obvious that she was still not completely recovered.

On December 16, 2010, representatives from the South Georgia Regional Prevention Coalition came to Kelsey's school to present her with an achievement award in the school's media center. The principal, first grade teacher, EIP math teacher, and EIP reading teacher were present and posed for pictures with Kelsey and her award. This award was significant and special to us because it was the first time Kelsey received an award. Who would have predicted that less than six years later she would be in Washington, DC, receiving a Prudential Spirit of Community Award for being recognized as one of the top ten youth volunteers in the nation?

On December 17, 2010, I attended the Christmas party in Kelsey's classroom at school from 2:30 to 3:30 p.m. For the first fifteen minutes of the party, the students presented a play with several parents and school staff (including the assistant principal and EIP reading teacher) in attendance. After the play concluded, school staff and most parents left. Other parents came in and out of the room during the remainder of the forty-five minutes. I was one of the only individuals who remained in the classroom the entire time.

During the last forty-five minutes of the party, I witnessed three students being hit, two being kicked and two male students rolling around on the floor fighting while attempting to choke each other and threatening to kill each other. No disciplinary measures (including verbal requests to stop the aggressive behavior) were employed.

In addition, I was concerned about the other incidents that were occurring. For example, at least two students were crying the majority of the time. One student was ignored by the teacher and was never comforted by the teacher during the forty-five minutes. Kelsey got under her desk and held her hands over her ears with her eyes closed, attempting to block out the chaos in the room. I have been told that Kelsey did this frequently throughout the school day that year when the chaos and violence in the classroom overwhelmed her. Keep in mind, weighing only thirty-five pounds, Kelsey was tiny compared to the other students in the room who were at least one foot taller than her and outweighed her by at least twenty-five pounds.

The teacher was busy eating the majority of the time during the class party. At one point, when the situation was out of control, she used her phone to call for assistance. At another point, she ran out of the room, shouting to the parents to watch the students because she had to go help another student. During this entire time, some parents were taking pictures and others were videoing the chaos. I have heard through the parent grapevine that these videos are on YouTube, although I have not seen them myself.

On December 28, 2010, I sent a copy of Kelsey's self-published book to the Houston county superintendent and chairperson of the Georgia State Board of Education. In the packet, I included a cover letter complimenting the EIP program teachers and speech therapy services. I also included pictures from Kelsey's award ceremony. In addition, I sent copies of the letter to her principal, assistant principal, EIP math teacher, EIP reading teacher, and speech therapist. They had done a terrific job and had been there to support Kelsey, at least some of the school day, when she was attempting to survive in the first grade classroom

On January 3, 2011, we held a meeting to discuss development of an informal behavior modification plan designed to address one issue (hitting and kicking). The meeting participants included the principal, assistant principals, guidance counselors, and Kelsey's private speech therapist who had been working with her since she was two years old. I reminded everyone that Kelsey had not started hitting anyone until after she was repeatedly hit, kicked, punched, and thrown against the classroom wall by some of the other students. They were over a foot taller than her and outweighed her by at least twenty-five pounds, and she was scared for her life. She was developmentally delayed and had the intelligence of a prekindergarten student. She was imitating what the developmentally older and bigger students were doing to her.

We decided that the behavior modification plan would be positive in nature (with no negative repercussions for not achieving the daily goal). The day was divided into nine segments (morning work, word study/spelling, writer's workshop, math calendar/math, lunch/recess, read aloud/guided reading, specials, science/social studies, and transitions). Kelsey would receive a smiley face sticker for each time segment she had with no hitting or kicking. The initial daily goal was to receive five out of ten stickers. Her first grade teacher was expected to award the stickers earned after each individual time segment each day. This was documented in a "My Success Notebook" that Kelsey was supposed to bring home daily. I was expected to sign it each evening and return it to school. The plan was supposed to last from January 4 to 26, 2011. This included a total of fourteen school days. Kelsey met her goal a total of twelve of the fourteen days (86 percent). Her average daily rating was seven points out of a possible nine.

On January 20, 2011, the assistant principal visited Kelsey's classroom and complimented her in front of her teacher and the other students for how well she was doing on her daily behavior modification plan. After hearing that she was planning on doing this, I became scared that her teacher was going to retaliate because she did not like Kelsey receiving compliments. As I predicted, less than five minutes after the assistant principal left the classroom, the first grade teacher reported that Kelsey was in trouble for throwing lip gloss.

On January 21, 2011, we held Kelsey's annual IEP update meeting. The participants included the school's speech therapist, occupational therapist, assistant principal, ESOL (English as a Second Language) instructional coach, and the first grade teacher. The occupational therapist told everyone that Kelsey was doing great in occupational therapy, and she had not observed any of the sensory related behaviors that the first grade teacher described. I reminded everyone that Kelsey was lactose intolerant and could not handle certain foods. When she eats certain foods, she will have uncontrollable diarrhea. Also, Kelsey gets frequent urinary tract infections (due to the medical issues associated with having Rubenstein-Taybi syndrome) and, often, the first indication that she is sick is when she has uncontrollable wetting accidents. In addition, I reminded the meeting's participants that, due to her Rubenstein-Taybi syndrome, Kelsey is physically smaller than the other students. However, her teeth are regularly sized and are too big for her mouth. Kelsey has had major dental issues as her permanent teeth have grown in and subsequently many have needed to be removed. Consequently, Kelsey is frequently in pain. I asked everyone to be aware of this so we could prevent avoidable disciplinary referrals resulting from her health issues.

On January 26, 2011, I contacted her principal and received permission to visit the classroom starting at 2:30 p.m. I arrived at 2:30 p.m. and observed the class. The first grade teacher handed the students a piece of paper with a hundred blank lines on it. She announced that, because it was the hundredth day of the school year, she wanted them to write a hundred words they had learned in first grade as fast as they could on the paper before it was time to stop. Several of the students looked at her with total confusion and bewilderment. One of the boys said, "This is too hard." She replied, "I have always made my students do this worksheet on the hundredth day of school and my students are always going to be expected to complete this worksheet in my classroom." She seemed to be looking straight at me when she said this.

I was astounded at this interaction because less than two months prior, she had been sitting in the principal's office with us receiving advice on how to appropriately interact with students with sensory disorders. She had been instructed to break her assignments up into smaller tasks given one at a time so students would not be overwhelmed. She had promised us that she would go back to the classroom and immediately start interacting with Kelsey in this manner by making tasks shorter and straightforward. Giving Kelsey a blank sheet of paper with a hundred lines and telling her to write a hundred words as fast as she can before the time is up is a total contradiction to this approach.

Several of the students gave up after approximately five minutes and stopped trying to write words on the paper. Kelsey was one of the students who was too overwhelmed to continue the assignment. Consequently, several of the children were misbehaving and the teacher addressed the issues with them. At the end of the day, while the teacher was busy writing in each student's agenda, a large heavy male student walked up to Kelsey and continued to push her hard on her back. The teacher ignored the entire episode and did not say anything to the male student. He pushed Kelsey at least four times causing her to move about 3/4 the width of the classroom. The final push caused her to fall hard to the floor. When Kelsey looked up from the floor, I motioned for Kelsey to come to me. After making sure that she was not hurt, I told her to return to her seat and ignore the male student. Kelsey complied and we left the classroom when school was dismissed for the day.

*****

When we arrived home, I went to my room and shut the door (so Kelsey could not see me) and cried. My daughter was being punched, kicked, hit and thrown to the ground and against the class-room walls, and no one was willing to do anything about it. I had complained repeatedly to the principal and begged him to remove her from that classroom, but he kept saying that he had no evidence that Kelsey was being physically harmed. I guess the bruises on her arms, legs, and torso area that stayed on her body from the first week of school until summer break were not enough evidence. I felt as if my daughter was being assaulted on a daily basis (by students and adults), and then punished when she attempted to protect herself. My biggest regret during her first grade year was that I did not contact the Georgia Professional Standards Commission (who is responsible for investigating potential improper conduct in Georgia's schools) and local law enforcement and attempt to press criminal charges for what was going on in that classroom.

Throughout her first grade experience, I felt guilty. As far as the school's administrators and staff were concerned, I was just another parent of a special education student who was struggling to survive at their school. However, I realized that I was that and much more. By that stage in my career, I was considered one of the leading con-sultants in the nation working with school systems that were pro-viding social and emotional support services for at-risk students. I routinely evaluate school-based early intervention programs such as social services, mental health, behavioral health, physical health, intensive tutoring, and afterschool programming and bullying prevention initiatives. During the past twenty-five years, I have spent thousands of hours evaluating these types of school-based programs that work with at-risk students who are struggling academically and/ or behaviorally. During my consulting work, I have sat in classrooms of schools throughout Georgia spending hundreds of hours observing and evaluating the manner in which staff members interact and support students. I can state with certainty that the situations I observed in Kelsey's first grade classroom and related meetings showcased the weakest classroom management skills and professional judgment that I have ever witnessed. As you can tell from reading the last two chapters, I keep meticulous notes and documentation about Kelsey's daily life. I have an entire file cabinet full of documentation regarding her kindergarten and first grade experiences. Yet despite my extensive experience and strong documentation skills, I could do nothing to improve the situation in that classroom and help my own daughter.

*****

On January 26, 2011, an article entitled "Bonaire First Grader Honored for Academics" was published by the *Macon Telegraph*. While I was proud of Kelsey and her accomplishments, I dreaded her going to school the next day because I had a gut feeling that her teacher and her friends were not going to let this go without retaliating. What happened was worse than I could have ever imagined.

*****

On January 27, 2011, I was notified by voice mail that Kelsey has been suspended from school for kicking three first grade teachers. Apparently, Kelsey was disciplined by the substitute teacher by not being allowed to go to specials. Another teacher volunteered to stay with her in the classroom while Kelsey's class went to specials. Kelsey did not come to her when requested and when the teacher attempted to grab Kelsey, Kelsey kicked her. Two additional teachers happened to allegedly be walking by the room and decided to help the first teacher by simultaneously cornering and physically grabbing Kelsey like a caged animal. All three teachers asserted that Kelsey kicked them during the incident. All three of these teachers are part of the group that attended Kelsey's last student support team meeting and stood up in unison and left the room while I was speaking. Kelsey came home crying and told me that they frightened her and hurt her bruised and swollen arms when they grabbed her and one of them told her that she was a bad girl and she needed to stop crying and stop asking for her mom. At that point, I was shaking in fear for my daughter and the injustice that was occurring against developmentally delayed students at that school. I wondered where the special education and English as a Second Language (ESOL) departments were and why they were not stepping in to protect my daughter from this abuse. At that time, Kelsey was considered a special education and an ESOL student and should have been under their protection. The lack of diversity and compassion was a major factor in the culture of the school, and the disabled and special needs students were suffering because of it.

The irony of this sad situation was that the substitute was in the classroom for the day because her first grade teacher was sent to a workshop to learn how to work with students with sensory issues and related developmental delays. What happened that day was evidence that every first grade teacher in the school needed to attend the same training.

I spoke to education experts including special education teachers who told me that the way they attempted to discipline Kelsey that day was the complete opposite of how teachers are supposed to handle developmentally delayed students (especially tiny thirty-five-pound girls who are the size of a three-year-old preschool student).

*****

One of the only things that kept our spirits up and hope alive during that year was Kelsey's continued involvement with a variety of community-based activities. Each afternoon, I would pick Kelsey up from school and watch her cry as she told me about what had happened at school that day. She had bruises on her arms, legs, and torso the entire school year. Sometimes, she even had bruises and marks on her face and neck. No one seemed to care but me. The principal ignored my complaints about the abuse that continued to occur in her classroom. Each afternoon, I would hold back my tears because I did not want Kelsey to see me cry. I would drive her to her regularly scheduled after-school activities such as dance, gymnastics, swimming, and cheerleading. During those few hours each afternoon, Kelsey would be treated as a human being and as an equal to every other child participating in that activity. For a couple of hours each day, she was happy and was able to interact with her peers in an environment that was free of chaos, violence, and ridicule. It was reassuring for me to watch her coaches and other adult volunteers treat her with respect and kindness. They gave me faith that the world did still have positive caring adults in it.

*****

I could go on and on with what transpired the remainder of the school year. I do not want to spend the entire book talking about Kelsey's first grade experience. Needless to say, it was a nightmare for both of us. The sad reality is that Kelsey told me she wanted to get sent to the ISS classroom each day because the teacher there would make sure that no one would hurt her. She said that the ISS teacher was nice and would help her with her reading and math. She told Kelsey that she could do it if she tried hard and would complement her when she did a good job. This was something Kelsey was not getting in her first grade classroom unless the EIP math or reading teachers happened to be there. No student should look forward to going to ISS just so they can be safe and be taught in a professional manner. Students should not have to worry about their physical safety while they are at school. Furthermore, routinely publically ridiculing a student in front of her classmates and other teachers is a hideous form of emotional abuse. This type of abuse can scar an individual for life.

*****

I couldn't sleep at night because I was so worried about Kelsey's safety and general well-being at that school. I would walk by her classroom during the day just to be certain that she wasn't lying on the floor somewhere hurt. I witnessed other students throwing desks, chairs, and books. I heard the teacher yelling and screaming at them. One time, she turned around and saw me and stopped yelling in mid-sentence. It was complete and total chaos.

At one point, I felt the only recourse that I had was to contact an attorney and pursue legal action to protect Kelsey. Through my research, I discovered that some of the other parents were just as upset as I was and had already threatened litigation. I spoke to several colleagues from other school systems in the state to obtain their advice. I was warned that, if I pursued litigation, I needed to remove Kelsey from the local school system the day before the lawsuit was filed to avoid retaliation. I couldn't protect her because I had to leave her alone with them during the school day. Then, suddenly, the Lord answered my prayers. Another parent informed me that the first grade teacher was being removed from the classroom at the end of the school year and put in a kindergarten classroom where she would always have another adult (paraprofessional) in the room with her. The first grade teacher had been warned that she was being watched, and Kelsey just needed to stick it out until the end of first grade.

In the meantime, I was advised to have a mental health professional do a psychological assessment on Kelsey to measure her IQ and test her for ADHD and autism. She had already been diagnosed as a toddler as having a rare genetic disorder called Rubenstein-Taybi syndrome. Individuals with the disorder have communication delays, are short (females don't typically grow to be taller than four foot eleven inches tall) and are at greater risk of developing a wide range of health problems such as cancer, heart problems, and digestive problems. The new testing documented that Kelsey has ADHD and is on the autism spectrum. She also has intellectual disabilities and was functioning, at the time, on the prekindergarten level. It was amazing that she was reading and handling math problems as well as she was. In essence, Kelsey was overachieving academically and was in the worst possible classroom situation with Early Intervention students, some of whom had serious behavior issues. The school system should never have put her in the first grade Early Intervention classroom with an inadequate teacher without my knowledge and permission. The tragedy that unfolded that year was a result of poor communication, incompetence, and the wrong placement of a student. One of the happiest days that I have experienced as a parent was on her last day of school in the first grade. Kelsey and I walked out of the school knowing that she would never again be left alone in that classroom.

The psychologist who tested Kelsey volunteered to attend her IEP meeting to decide where to place Kelsey for the upcoming second grade school year. Unfortunately, the principal did not want to schedule that IEP meeting until after the new school year began in September 2011. In preparation for the meeting, I met with various experts to ask their advice and guidance. Every one of them told me that it was required by federal law to place Kelsey in the least restrictive environment possible so she could thrive academically. We all assumed that meant in a general education classroom with appropriate accommodations and supports (including, if necessary, her own paraprofessional). Because I am not a special education expert, I asked a friend, JoEllen Harden, who is a retired special education director from another school system to attend the IEP meeting with me. What transpired at that meeting shocked me to my core as a parent. Immediately after we sat down at the meeting, I was informed by the meeting's facilitator that Kelsey would not be going to a general education classroom at that school. They had decided that she needed to be placed immediately into a self-contained special education classroom without giving her an opportunity to try a lesser restrictive environment. When my friend and I attempted to reason with them and point out federal law, we were told they were unwilling to consider that option. They also mentioned, more than once, that since Kelsey was already struggling in first grade, she was likely not to do well on the state's standardized tests when she was in third grade. I knew the school had a reputation of quickly identifying any student who was at risk of not doing well on the standardized tests and moving them into the special education classroom and designating them for the alternative assessment so they would not negatively impact the school's test scores report; however, it was hard to watch my child be a victim of this practice. The public elementary school was proud of its status of having some of the best standardized test scores in the county. In fact, Kelsey's kindergarten principal had bragged that "we are the best private school option in Houston County" because only a handful of their students do not meet the state testing standards each year. The meeting ended abruptly after the facilitator told me that my daughter would be going directly to a self-contained special education classroom and it did not matter what I thought because they knew my daughter's abilities better than I did.

I was very upset and shocked that federal law was not being followed. I was scared that Kelsey was going to receive additional negative retaliatory treatment at school, but I wanted to effectively advocate for her future. I read the Americans with Disabilities Act (ADA) document that I had been given that outlined my rights as a parent regarding special education. I prayed and then I called the number at the Georgia Department of Education to report a potential violation of my daughter's rights. The person whom I spoke with at the Georgia Department of Education was sympathetic and said that the IEP meeting could be reconvened and that I had every right to insist upon the least restrictive environment for my daughter. She said that she would call the local school system and tell them to schedule another meeting.

I was not prepared for the volcanic explosion that occurred after the school system was notified. The school system's special education representative who had facilitated the original meeting said that she wanted to meet with me immediately back at the school. I got in my car and drove back to the school by myself. She was waiting for me in a meeting room and started yelling at me. She said that I had no right to contact the state and complain about her. She said that she doesn't tolerate anyone getting her in trouble with her boss. I was in shock. I had no idea that a school system employee would be allowed to talk to me like this. More importantly, however, I felt defeated and scared to death for the safety and well-being of my daughter. I realized that I had two realistic choices: (1) back down and allow my child to be placed directly into a self-contained special education classroom, or (2) immediately remove her from the local school system and try to enroll her somewhere else. I left the school crying that day.

After much thought and prayer, I decided to allow Kelsey to go to the self-contained classroom. There were several reasons for doing this. First, I knew the special education teacher. She had been Kelsey's private tutor and was a big reason why Kelsey continued to do so well academically. She was a very good teacher and was kind, compassionate, and cared about her students. The second reason was that Kelsey was physically afraid to enter the school building at the beginning of second grade. She was still traumatized by what had happened in first grade. Her physical bruises had started to fade, but the emotional scars were still there. I knew that the special education teacher would keep her safe, and when I spoke to her, she promised me that she would not allow anyone to hurt or abuse Kelsey. I trusted her to keep her promise and she did.

The other reason I made my decision to allow Kelsey to go into the special education classroom was that I was physically and mentally exhausted from fighting. I had always been in perfect health. Until then, the only times I ever was a patient in a hospital was to remove my tonsils in third grade and to remove my gallbladder in my early thirties. During Kelsey's first grade year, I started having tremendous stress headaches and other health issues. Less than one year after all of the first grade classroom drama, I collapsed on my way to pick up Kelsey from school. I was in a coma for several days with the doctors telling me, after I had recovered, that the stress I was put under during Kelsey's first grade experience was a significant factor in me getting sick and almost dying. I will share more details about the health scare in a later chapter.

Since making that decision in the fall of 2011 to allow Kelsey to be placed in a self-contained special education environment, I have prayed every night that it was the right decision. I am still haunted by the lingering doubt that it was actually the right decision. Sometimes, I wake in the middle of the night and lie in bed second-guessing myself for the remainder of the night.

During Kelsey's tenure at the elementary school, I learned what it was like to be a parent of a developmentally disabled student. I realized that it is a multi-tiered system (similar to an upstairs-versus-downstairs situation). The general education students are on the first tier (upstairs), which is on an even playing field, and they are encouraged to excel academically, participate in extracurricular activities, and join clubs. The special education students are on the second tier (downstairs situation) kept in self-contained classrooms where they are segregated from the general school population for most of the day. At one point, the principal suggested that I enroll Kelsey in a private school if I wanted her to participate in additional activities. Another administrator told me that it was hard to deal with special education parents because so many of us have our own developmental disabilities. I finally realized that they expected special education parents to accept our preordained place in the school infrastructure, and if we kept quiet, our children would be treated better.

Families should not be forced into this position. We are taxpayers (who finance and pay the salaries of public school system employees), and we should expect equal and just treatment for our children. No parent should be threatened, intimidated, retaliated against, or made to feel guilty for advocating for what her child needs. We need to have supporters and advocates who are willing to help us fight for our children's futures.

CHAPTER 6

Special Education Environment

Kelsey began to immediately thrive with her special education teacher's encouragement and support. Kelsey looked forward to going to school and actually started smiling again. Starting in second grade, she soared academically and socially without me having to fight for her to be treated like a human being (instead of a piece of unwanted garbage). To date, Kelsey has been a student in the local school system for ten years. The only times she has had any disciplinary issues and sent to ISS was in first grade. There has never been an incident since then.

It took Kelsey several years to overcome the damage that had been inflicted in first grade. Unfortunately, she will carry the emotional scars with her for the remainder of her life. Thankfully, starting in second grade, she had wonderful teachers who were trained to teach students using individualized instruction. I am grateful for those special education teachers who not only taught Kelsey how to read and write, but also taught her that school can be a kind and supportive place that values human dignity and the potential that exists for every child, no matter their disability.

Kelsey remained enrolled at the local elementary school from second to fifth grade. She had three different special education teachers during elementary school. All of these individuals were wonderful and a complete and total contrast to what she and other developmentally delayed students experienced in the general education environment at that school.

While I was happy that Kelsey was being treated like a human being, I began to become concerned about other issues. For example, at every annual IEP meeting, I brought up the fact that Kelsey needed to have extracurricular options at school. I suggested that she be allowed to join the school chorus or the school dance team. I was told that it would not be possible because the regular education teachers who were responsible for those activities did not have time to include special education students.

I also asked about the Special Olympics. They said that the school system had Special Olympics events planned in the spring and the summer, that all special education students could participate in activities such as bouncing balls, throwing softballs, walking, and running. I told them that I was not talking about special activities. Instead, I was talking about competing in gymnastics and swimming. I told them that Kelsey had been training in gymnastics since she was two and swimming for the local swim team since she was in early elementary school. I told them that I knew there were state Special Olympics competitions in Atlanta, and I wanted her to compete. Her dream has always been to participate in the World Special Olympics games as a member of Team USA, and she is never going to get there without competing at the state level. Each year, they referred me to the school system's Special Olympics coordinator who subsequently told me that Kelsey would not be allowed to do that. She said that the school system had a high school wheelchair basketball team and they were the only athletes allowed to represent the school system at the state Special Olympics competitions. She said that maybe Kelsey would have more opportunities regarding the state Special Olympics competitions once she entered high school. However, she warned me that the local school board would never approve of a special education student representing the school system in a state Special Olympics swimming competition because of the liability. I attempted to reason with her and explain that Kelsey competing at the state Special Olympics games would not cost the school system any money because I was already paying for her private coaches and I would pay for any travel and registration costs. When the answer was still no, I asked if I could speak to her supervisor, and, again, I was told this would not be possible.

Consequently, I had to use my savings to continue to enroll Kelsey in community-based extracurricular activities. After school, I drove her to gymnastics, dance, cheerleading, swim team practice, and horse-riding lessons. She never had any extracurricular options available for her and other special education students at the elementary school. This is unfortunate because special education students deserve to have the same rights and access to extracurricular activities as general education students. In addition, research has documented that when students with developmental disabilities are involved in extracurricular and social interaction—related activities starting in elementary school (or even earlier), they are more likely to develop into confident and independent adults capable of functioning in the general community. Waiting until high school before encouraging them to interact with their peers and become more social is a recipe for subsequent failure and a lifetime of social isolation. Furthermore, students with developmental disabilities are at greater risk of becoming overweight adults because of years of living a sedentary lifestyle due to lack of access to intramural and competitive athletic—related activities.

The other issue that I kept asking about during the annual IEP meetings was why the special education students did not receive grades. I was told repeatedly that Kelsey was doing great academically, but she would never receive grades while she was in the special education classroom at the elementary school. Consequently, she was never on the honor roll in elementary school and was never invited to attend school awards ceremonies. Again, this is a shame because students with developmental disabilities need to be taught that they can achieve their dreams by trying hard and doing well academically. We need to instill in them the confidence that they can go to college (or some type of post-secondary training program) with the proper assistance and support. They need to be recognized for their academic achievements starting in elementary school in the same manner as students who are in the general education environment.

Figure 27 Competing at the Miss Bonaire
Middle School Pageant in 8th Grade

The issue that concerned me in the fifth grade was when I found out that Kelsey and the other fifth grade special education students were not included in the fifth grade substance abuse/violence prevention classes that local law enforcement conducted. When I asked why, her fifth grade special education teacher told me that she was a relatively new teacher at the school and no one told her about the classes. This is a shame because research has documented that special education students are at greater risk of accidentally misusing or abusing substances (often because they do not know what they are) and being the victim of bullying and other violence. The special education students need this instruction even more than the general education students do. Unfortunately, Kelsey and her special education classmates transitioned from the local elementary school without this education and knowledge.

Everything changed when Kelsey entered the local middle school at the beginning of sixth grade. The middle school welcomed and encouraged special education students to become involved in the general school environment. For the first time, Kelsey had the opportunity to participate in a science fair, join school clubs, and was encouraged to attend the school dances. More importantly, Kelsey started to receive grades in her academic classes. Throughout middle school (sixth to eighth grades), she was a straight-A honor roll student and a member of the Junior Beta Club. She was invited to the annual awards night each year and received her well-deserved academic awards alongside her general education classmates as an equal. At the end of her eighth grade year, she received the Presidential Award for Academic Excellence signed by the president of the United States. This was pretty amazing considering the fact that her first

Figure 28 8th Grade
Photo credit: Bonnie Rebholz

grade teacher had labeled her as "dumb," "a bad girl," and "unable to be taught." We will be forever grateful for her exceptional special education teachers at her elementary and middle school and the administrators and general education teachers at her middle school. Good teachers make all the difference in the world!

As we are writing this book, Kelsey is getting ready to enter the local high school. We have high hopes and expectations. We have heard wonderful things about the high school and its excellent staff. However, in the back of our minds, we still remember the conflict and trauma from kindergarten and first grade and are always fearful when we enter a new academic environment until we are reassured about the quality, integrity, and compassion of the teaching staff.

The one thing that I know for certain is that Kelsey will be attending college, whether it is a regular degree program or a two-year certificate program. Currently, nine Georgia colleges and universities offer post secondary inclusion programs for students with developmental disabilities. Students who graduate from these programs are more likely to obtain gainful employment and live independently than their developmentally disabled peers.

CHAPTER 7

Health Scares

In December 2013, when Kelsey was in second grade, I was driving to pick her up from school. At some point, I started to pass out and pulled my car over to the curb while I was still in our neighborhood. A neighbor saw my car at the curb and looked in the car and saw me slumped against the wheel. My cell phone started ringing and she answered it. It was Kelsey's teacher calling because I had not shown up to pick her up from school. The lady who found me told her what happened and told her that she had just called 9-1-1 and the ambulance was on its way. Kelsey's teacher told her principal and she put Kelsey in her car and drove to the neighborhood. The principal followed her in his car. They arrived on the scene as the EMTs were loading me into the ambulance. Kelsey became upset when she saw me in that condition. The ambulance took me to the regional trauma center in Macon because they did not know, at that time, whether or not I was having a stroke or a heart attack.

Her principal drove my car to my house and put it in our garage and made certain the house was locked and secured. Kelsey's teacher took her back to the school and called the emergency number on Kelsey's emergency card. The number was for Kelsey's godparents who lived about forty-five minutes away in a neighboring county. They said that they were going to drive directly to the hospital but would send somebody to pick up Kelsey immediately and bring her home with them. However, they told her teacher that they could not bring her back and forth to school each day, and Kelsey would have to miss school for the remaining week of the semester. Her teacher said that it would not be necessary. With their permission, she took Kelsey home with her and Kelsey stayed with her for the next week until the school semester finished before Christmas break. I am grateful for Kelsey's teacher and principal who went well beyond the call of duty to keep Kelsey safe during this crisis situation.

Meanwhile, at the hospital, my condition was declining rapidly. I could still answer questions in the ambulance, but not long after arriving at the emergency department, I went into a coma. They conducted a battery of tests during the next couple of days to attempt to determine what was wrong with me. The ruled out a heart attack and stroke and did not find any drugs in my system. After numerous tests, they discovered that I was an undiagnosed diabetic and was in a diabetic coma. My condition continued to rapidly deteriorate and the doctors said that they needed to contact my family in Missouri to inform them that if they wanted to see me before I died they needed to get there immediately. The doctors told my friends that I was dying, and they did not expect me to recover. When my friends and family insisted that I was a fighter and could pull through, they told them that, even if I lived, I would probably have severe brain damage and would never be the same.

They called for a priest to give me last rites. My Methodist and Baptist friends said that they thought they could hear me saying the same prayer over and over again. A Catholic hospital employee told them that I must be trying to say the rosary because it sounded like I was trying to say the Hail Mary.

I have always wondered what it was like to be between life and death. I have read all kinds of stories and watched TV shows where people who had near-death experiences told about what had happened to them. I never thought it would happen to me. I don't remember much about what happened the day I collapsed. I remember leaving my house to pick up Kelsey, but that is all I remember about that day.

While I was in a coma, I had a very surreal experience. I thought I was on an airplane that had an all-white interior. Everything was gleaming like newly fallen snow. I was laying down on something in the middle of the airplane and I kept asking where we were going. No one would answer me. For some reason, I saw a sunrise or sunset out of the window of the plane. It is funny how your human brain doesn't understand at first what is happening to you and you try to rationalize it. I immediately thought my insurance company was too cheap to pay for my health care at the Macon hospital and was transporting me somewhere to a hospital on the Gulf Coast that was just beyond the horizon.

The next thing I knew, I was in a rowboat headed for the horizon. Again, I realized that I was on a journey, but it took me some time to realize that I wasn't going to another hospital; instead, we were on our way to heaven. I do not know who was with me, but I sensed that someone was right there. I kept telling anyone who would listen to me that we had to turn the boat around and get back to Macon. I told them that I wanted to go home because Kelsey was waiting for me there and would not understand why I was gone. I thought if I argued hard enough, I could convince them that I needed to go home.

At some point, I sensed that we stopped, and I was in some type of transition place where they were waiting for someone. For the first time, I heard a voice, and I thought I was talking to God. It might have been the priest giving me the last rites. I do not know for certain, but I suddenly didn't feel fear anymore, and I knew that I was going back home to Kelsey. The next thing I remember is seeing a light (like a light coming down a tunnel). I kept walking toward it and the next thing that happened is that I began to regain consciousness. The nurse had been shining a light in my eyes, and I suddenly shocked everyone by saying "Get that light out of my eyes." The next thing I knew, there was suddenly a lot of noise and commotion in the room as people started running in to see if I was really coming out of the coma.

They asked me a lot of questions like "Do you know your name?" "Do you have a child?" "What is her name?" At first, I didn't recognize the sound of my own voice. My voice sounded like that of a stroke victim who could not talk very well. At first, I could not move my arms or my legs, but I could feel someone poking my feet. It took me a couple of days to fully regain my voice and start to move my arms and legs. My hands felt like giant paws and I could not manipulate my fingers. One of my sisters, who is a physical therapist, told me that this was normal, and I needed to practice moving my fingers back and forth.

Everyone (especially my doctors) was shocked that I had recovered with no apparent brain damage. I was distressed to learn that my legs were not moving very well and I was too weak to walk. During the next several weeks, I had to learn how to walk again. The day that I stood up (with the help of a physical therapist and a walker) and took several steps outside of my hospital room, there were several doctors, nurses, and other staff members lining the hallway looking with amazement. They had not thought that this would be possible.

Kelsey and her godparents picked me up from the hospital on Christmas evening and took me home. They had arranged for someone to stay with Kelsey and me while I recuperated. I immediately started physical therapy through home health care and gradually worked my way up to being able to ride in a car to the physical therapy center to continue intensive outpatient physical therapy. Throughout my recuperation, I worked from home with my computer and printer. It was a several-month struggle, but I recovered. Throughout the entire ordeal, Kelsey was my motivation to keep trying to recover and get well.

After December 2013, I worked hard to eat right, take my insulin and control my blood sugar levels, lower my blood pressure, and get additional exercise. I had so much to live for and wanted to be around for a long time for Kelsey's sake. I vowed that something like this would never happen again.

Unfortunately, God had other plans. In the fall of 2016, I started to not feel right. I kept going back to my primary care physician's office and was examined numerous times by his nurse practitioner. She treated me for a urinary tract infection, but I would only feel good for a short time and would start feeling sick again. I know that they were tired of me complaining about not feeling well, but I was not getting better.

In March 2017, Kelsey and I were supposed to travel to Nashville for Kelsey to attend the National Youth Activist award ceremony. We started driving for Nashville, and I had to pull over because I felt sick to my stomach. A good Samaritan stopped and said that she was a nurse and that I looked like I needed to go to the hospital. I decided that we needed to cancel our trip, and we needed to return home. We arrived home and after I fed Kelsey dinner, I immediately sat in the recliner and covered myself with the heating blanket. I felt like I was freezing and I could not get warm. I do not know how much time had passed, but at some point, I passed out on the chair while Kelsey was taking a bath. She tried to wake me up, but I was unresponsive. Kelsey panicked and did not remember how to dial 9-1-1. She ran outside and tried to get the neighbor's attention. It was the middle of the night, and the neighbor saw her in the yard. They called 9-1-1, and they knew the number of her babysitter, Layne Fulghum, who lived in the neighborhood, so they called her. The ambulance picked me up and took me to the local medical center. Kelsey's babysitter took Kelsey home with her.

This time, the situation was even more serious than before. I stopped breathing in the emergency department and they had to put me on a ventilator. I went into a coma. I spent the next four weeks in the intensive care unit on the ventilator. They discovered that I had a urinary tract infection that spread to my other organs. I developed pneumonia and sepsis. All of my major organs started to shut down, including my kidneys that were only working at 3 percent. They brought a dialysis machine to my ICU room and put me on dialysis to attempt to save my life. Again, the doctors said that I was probably not going to make it and, once again, I proved them wrong. A priest was called once again to give me the last rites.

My second near-death experience was not nearly as peaceful as the first one had been. Along the journey, everyone kept telling me that I was going to heaven and that I should stop fighting to stay alive and just let go. I told them that I was going way too soon. I felt that Kelsey was in danger and needed me to get to her as soon as possible. I felt I needed to leave and go back the way that I had come, but no one would listen to me. I couldn't reason with them. I was very agitated and felt that I was fighting to stay alive and to return to Kelsey. When I regained consciousness in my ICU room, I was exhausted from fighting and could not speak because of the ventilator. It seemed like an eternity that day while they were waiting for my condition to stabilize before they took me off of the ventilator.

I was right to be worried. It seemed like the minute that I could talk, I had people lined up to talk to me. My friends, Kelsey's babysitter, and my administrative assistant from work all needed to talk to me immediately. They told me that the doctors were going to be mad that they were upsetting me, but I needed to know about Kelsey. They told me that when they called my family to tell them that I was in the hospital, it took one of my sisters a while to show up at the hospital. She only stayed a few days and, while she was there, she refused to meet with Kelsey to comfort her. During those days, she told people that she really didn't know Kelsey that well, and she wasn't really related to her. She did not want to raise a special needs orphan and suggested that Kelsey be put into the foster system if I died. She left Georgia to return home after abandoning responsibility for Kelsey. Her excuse for needing to leave so soon was that her son had golf practice and her daughter's sorority was having a mother-daughter party. It seemed as if activities like golf and sorority parties were more important to her than protecting a child whose mother might be dying.

I asked them to get me my cell phone. I immediately called my sister from my ICU bed, and she was surprised that I was still alive. She was even more surprised when I told her what I had been told about her behavior toward Kelsey. She became defensive and hung up on me. The next thing I know is that I received an email from her (that I read on my cell phone from my hospital bed in the ICU) informing me that she was relinquishing her responsibilities as executer of my estate and told me to revise my will. She also said, in writing, that she had no interest in raising Kelsey and neither did any of my other siblings and family members. I received a second email a few minutes later from one of my other sisters who informed me that she was relinquishing her responsibilities making medical decisions on my behalf if I am in a health crisis and told me to revise my health care advance directives document. It is not surprising that, after reading these two email messages, my vital signs and overall health condition started to deteriorate again.

I laid in that hospital bed not knowing if I was going to recover. The doctors had just told me that my kidneys were only functioning at 3 percent, and they did not know if they would ever work properly without dialysis. The cardiologist told me that my heart was being carefully monitored for the next several days. I could not move my legs and I realized, based on what I went through to recover the first time that I was in a coma, that it would be a long recovery road ahead. I had to make a decision that day in the hospital bed. I could have given up and decided to die, but I knew that Kelsey was counting on me, and I also had a business to run that supported us and paid for our health insurance. I decided that giving up or not getting well was not an option. I decided to fight with every ounce of my being. I got on my cell phone and contacted my attorney and told him he needed to get to the hospital as soon as possible because I needed a new will and a health care advance directives document to protect Kelsey in case anything happened to me while I was in the hospital.

I spoke to the hospital social worker and tried to get placed in a rehabilitation program so I could recover more quickly than trying to do it by myself. Unfortunately, my insurance company would not pay for rehabilitation because they considered me too weak and medically unstable to actually recover. I then went to plan B, which included making arrangements to go home with a hospital bed and physical therapy services provided by home health care and coordinate my own recovery. I also needed to receive dialysis treatments to hopefully coax my kidneys into deciding to work again. That meant that I had to arrange for a nonemergency transportation ambulance to take me to and from my outpatient dialysis appointments on a stretcher because I couldn't walk yet.

It also meant that I need to start working full-time again to keep my company going and pay the bills. I had my computer from work set up at home so I could work from home the day the ambulance brought me home. After several dialysis treatments, my kidneys started working again. After several weeks of home-based physical therapy, I was able to walk well enough with a walker to go to outpatient physical therapy services. After several months of hard work at the physical therapy center, I learned to walk again with a cane and sometimes with a rolling walker (for longer distances). I didn't bounce back as fast as I did the first time. In fact, even two years later, I still have some residual effects like not being able to walk long distances without my rolling walker. I have learned and accepted what it is like to be physically disabled. My mind and inner drive are still there as sharp as ever; however, my legs may never be fully mobile again.

We will never be able to thank the wonderful circle of friends who supported us during these health scares. Layne Fulghum and her family; Kat Quick; Nancy, Mike, and Melissa Peacock; Julie Kozyreva; the Willard family; Pam Lashley and her family; Mrs. Sally and the staff at KidsAmerica; Rachel Jenkins; Joshua Hirsch; Kim Smith; Rebecca Banks; Edward Davis; Cora Bobo; Debbie Connell; Regina Smith; Gloria Pylant; Brenda Lee; Dianne Huff; Wanda Davis; Becky Anderson; the Ondike family; the Register family; the Quattlebaum family; the Schoonover family; my other clients; Kelsey's teachers; and many others. If I have left someone's name off, it is unintentional. We will always be grateful for their support and friendship.

Throughout these health scares and the last two years recovering from them, I have been reminded what is really important in life. Kelsey needs me. I am the only family she has and I need to be around a long time for her as she matures into adulthood. I know other people think and talk about big vacations they want to take and places they want to travel to see. I spend my time thinking about Kelsey's future and thanking God every day for allowing me to continue to stay on this earth to take care of her.

CHAPTER 8

Kelsey and Her Dogs

Figure 29 Kelsey and Izzie on the trampoline
Photo credit: Tamara Joiner

I think the most significant turning point in Kelsey's life was the day she met her dog, Izzie. Since second grade, Izzie has been her protector, best friend, and confidant. They were joined a few years later by an abandoned puppy named Sadie. It has been the power of this bond, cemented by mutual love, that has forever changed Kelsey's life.

Kelsey has always loved animals. I remember on my first visit to the Russian orphanage when I met Kelsey, there were a few worn posters on the wall in the room where Kelsey and the other orphans were housed. None of the orphanage workers spoke English, and I needed to bring a translator with me in order to communicate with them. One of the workers said she wanted to show me something. She looked at Kelsey and said "cat" in Russian and Kelsey immediately smiled and clapped her hands and pointed to the poster. At that point, she had never seen a real cat but she had decided she liked them.

*****

During my first several hours with Kelsey at the orphanage, I held her tightly and sang to her in English. She looked at me like I was some type of foreign space alien who was speaking in a strange language. The song she liked that I was singing over and over again was "Mary Had a Little Lamb." She smiled every time I started to sing the song again.

Once we arrived home in Georgia, we immediately started her stuffed animal collection. Our house soon became full of all types of stuffed animals. She preferred the stuffed animals over her dolls. Her first favorite stuffed animal was a little pink lamb she named Rosie. During her first couple of years at home, she carried Rosie everywhere she went.

As much as she loved her stuffed animals, she loved real ones even more. Every time she saw a puppy or a cat, she wanted to pet and hold them. By the time she was four, she was begging me just about every day to buy her a puppy. I wanted to wait until she

Figure 30 Kelsey with her first stuffed animal Rosie the lamb

was older and could start taking care of a pet before we introduced one into our household. That strategy worked until she started experiencing the heartbreaking bullying episodes during first grade. Every night she came home from school with bruises, crying and feeling like she did not have a friend in the world. It helped that she was very busy after school in a variety of extracurricular community activities, including cheerleading, gymnastics, and dance. During those community-based activities, she interacted with many children and had many friends she looked forward to interacting with each week. However, something was still missing in her life.

When she turned eight, I decided it was time to begin looking for a dog. I did not want to buy one from a store. I wanted to find just the right rescue dog that needed a good home. One of my friends, Debbie, sent me a picture of a rescue dog named Izzie that was looking for a loving home. Izzie was approximately seven months old and was being fostered by a family of dog lovers. Apparently, a good Samaritan almost ran over Izzie when she was approximately six weeks old on an isolated rural Georgia road. Someone had dumped her along the side of the road and left her to die. He stopped and put Izzie in his car and drove her to the family's house that he knew would take care of her. Several months later, that family realized it was time for Izzie to find her forever home and distributed her picture, encouraging someone to adopt her.

Figure 31 Kelsey meeting Izzie in December 2011

*****

When I saw Izzie's picture, I told Debbie that I was very interested and wanted to meet Izzie. After meeting Izzie a few days later, I decided that she would be perfect for our family. The next Saturday, when Kelsey was home from school, I took Kelsey to meet Izzie and bring her home. I think it was the happiest day of Kelsey's life.

At that time, she was still not very verbal. She had been working with speech therapists for several years. They had made progress but Kelsey still wasn't spending much time speaking in complete sentences to other people. When she met Izzie for the first time, her face lit up like a Christmas tree. She hugged her and would not let go of her the entire forty-five-minute drive home.

Figure 32 Kelsey bringing Izzie home in December 2011

When we arrived home, Kelsey showed Izzie every room in the entire house and then took her outside in the backyard to play. The backyard became their kingdom. We have a big backyard (approximately 1 acre) that has a six-foot-tall wooden privacy/security fence surrounding it. There are plenty of trees, a swing set, an enclosed pool, and a big enclosed trampoline. The two of them spent hours every day after school and on weekends exploring the backyard and playing imaginary games. Kelsey decided that Izzie was her BFF (best friend forever). Their most favorite place to play in the backyard was Kelsey's trampoline. Kelsey loved jumping on it and Izzie soon learned to jump with her. I became so accustomed to seeing them jump together

Figure 33 Kelsey playing in the back yard with Izzie

that it seemed very natural to me. Other adults, however, who saw them jumping together for the first time always were shocked to see a dog jumping on her hind legs like a human with a smile on her face.

The most amazing thing about their friendship, however, was the immediate change in Kelsey. She would spend hours sitting on the trampoline with Izzie reading to her. Kelsey took her story books outside to the trampoline every afternoon, and they would read together until it was too dark to see the pages. Kelsey would also talk to Izzie in complete sentences telling her about her day at school and talking about what she wanted to do when she grew up.

One of the most touching things that Kelsey and Izzie did each evening was to pray together. Kelsey spent hours teaching Izzie the prayers and Bible verses that she was learning in Sunday school. Kelsey would repeat them over and over again to Izzie until Kelsey had memorized them. Then, every evening, Kelsey would pray with Izzie, and while Kelsey was reciting the Lord's Prayer, Izzie would bow her head. It seemed as if Izzie was also praying. I cried every time I watched them together. Izzie quickly became an integral part of our family.

The most frightening day of my life occurred on Friday, January 27, 2012. Kelsey loved to play with Izzie when she came home from school (especially on Friday nights because she did not have any of her extracurricular activities after school). I keep all of our doors locked with the exception of the back door when Kelsey is in the backyard playing. There are three gates to the backyard that are always kept padlocked. When the pool or yard people needed to get into the backyard, they have to knock on the front door and ask me to unlock one of the gates. I am the only person who has keys to the backyard gates.

On that Friday afternoon, Kelsey and Izzie were playing in the backyard, and I went into the house to answer the phone. Kelsey's teacher was calling me with good news about a test Kelsey took at school earlier that day. We talked for—fifteen to twenty minutes and I went back outside to feed Izzie. When I walked outside the back door, I could not find Kelsey and Izzie. They were not in the backyard. Since I thought that there was no other way to get out of the backyard other than to come into the house, I immediately assumed that somehow I had not seen them when they decided to come back into the house. I searched the first floor of the house and could not find them. I then assumed that they must be upstairs playing in Kelsey's room. When I checked, there was no one upstairs. I immediately methodically searched every room in the house, including all closets and the garage. They were not in the house. Then I looked through the back window and saw the pool. I immediately panicked because, in my mind, that was the only other place they could be. By that time, it was starting to get dark, and I had to turn on the pool lights to look into the pool. Thank goodness, they were not there.

By that time, I had run out of options regarding where to look. They had vanished. I could not figure out how they had been able to leave the backyard. Even though I knew that it was highly unlikely that they were in the front yard or anywhere else in the neighborhood, I ran around the front yard and down the street calling their names. No one helped me or expressed any concern regarding a missing child. At that point, I called 9-1-1 and told them that there was a special needs child and her dog that were missing. After getting a description of Kelsey and Izzie, the 9-1-1 operator told me to stay at home and wait for the sheriff's deputies. I also called Kelsey's godparents (Nancy and Mike). Mike was the police chief in Butler, Georgia, which is about a one-hour drive away. Nancy told me that they were on their way to help. Afterward, Nancy told me that within five minutes of my call, Mike had his car loaded with his guns, search gear, big flashlights, and some type of search spotlight.

While I was waiting for everyone to arrive, I kept running around the backyard and the front of the house calling Kelsey's name. Just after the sun went down, I thought I heard a child crying and a dog barking. At first, it was very faint and it started to get louder and it seemed like it was coming from the back of the house. I ran into the backyard screaming Kelsey's name. It was very dark and I could only see a few yards in front of me. Just then, Izzie ran toward me and Kelsey was running behind her crying for me. They both were soaked from head to toe and they were covered in mud. They both were very upset.

After questioning Kelsey, we determined that Izzie had dug a hole under the fence at the back of our property and climbed under it. Kelsey was worried about Izzie and followed her under the fence. Kelsey said that, at some point, she fell into a "swamp" and was lying in the water and could not get up. Izzie, apparently, kept trying to grab the fabric of her pink Disney princess sweatshirt with her teeth. The scratch and teeth marks on Kelsey's right shoulder supported Kelsey's story. Izzie was pulling on the fabric around the shoulder and hood of her sweatshirt to get Kelsey to stand up and get out of the water. Kelsey said she could not find her way home because all she saw were fences. (Many of my neighbors have the same type of six-foot fence that we have.) Kelsey said that she followed Izzie, and Izzie stopped at one of the fences and started to dig under the fence. She followed Izzie under the fence, and it was into our backyard.

The most frightening aspect of this scenario is that the landscape changes a few feet from our back property line. There is some type of a drop-off into a gully with running water (after it rains). Kelsey must have fallen into the gully. There are no houses behind us because we adjoin the 19,200-acre Oaky Woods Wildlife Management Area. It is supposed to have bobcats, foxes, black bears, wild hogs, snakes, beavers, otters, and panthers. If Izzie had not found her way back to our yard, they would probably have been in the habitat at least for the night. I do not think that the search parties would have been able to do much in the dark in that terrain. If not for Izzie's protective instincts, Kelsey probably would have died that night.

Kelsey was pretty shaken up and was freezing when I found her. I declined an ambulance for her because she seemed okay and would have become more upset if she had to leave home to go to the hospital. After a hot bath (for both her and Izzie), she calmed down and talked to us. Nancy and Mike stayed a while to talk to her and make certain she was all right. Mike walked the perimeter of our fence with a flashlight and found the place on the fence line where they came back into the yard. He said he could see the claw marks that Kelsey made with her hands and shoes as she was frantically digging through the dirt and mud to follow Izzie back into the yard. He told me to get an invisible fence for Izzie that will not allow her to get close enough to the big fence to dig. The next day, I contacted our lawn service company to fill in the holes under the fence so Kelsey could get out again. I also made arrangements to have an invisible fence installed.

Kelsey had some scratches on her legs and hands, but she was okay. She went to her cheerleading game on Saturday and Sunday school on Sunday. Kelsey seemed fine, but it took me several days to calm down. We almost lost her that Friday evening.

Figure 34 Kelsey and Sadie buying a sweater

Our family seemed fairly complete, except we began to worry that Izzie might be lonely. As Kelsey grew older, she spent more time at dance performances, practices, pageants, and working on community service projects. She no longer had several hours each afternoon to play with Izzie. We decided that we needed to find a friend for Izzie and started looking for a rescue puppy that would fit into our family.

Right before Christmas, one of our friends posted a picture on Facebook asking if anyone was looking for a puppy. We went to meet the puppies that her sister was fostering. There were several puppies in the litter. Their mother had

Figure 35 The Norris girls

been a stray who was shot by someone who left the puppies to die.

A rescue group found them, and they were being cared for by a foster family. There was one female in the litter who had already been named Sadie. She was feisty and friendly. She was the smallest puppy in the litter and fought her brothers for a place at the food bowl.

Kelsey immediately fell in love with her and wanted to bring her home. Sadie was barely six weeks old, and Kelsey was scared to put her down on the floor. I will never forget when the two dogs met each other on our kitchen floor. Izzie came running into the room when we arrived home that night with Sadie. She did not know what to think. She will never have puppies of her own (she had the operation before we adopted her), and I worried that she would not know how to act around a new puppy. Izzie immediately sniffed Sadie and decided that she would become her mother. From that day forward, the two dogs were inseparable. Sadie followed Izzie everywhere. They slept together, ate together, and played together. The only time they ever became irritated with each other was when one of them thought that Kelsey was giving the other dog too much attention. They both wanted to sit on Kelsey's lap or cuddle with her on the coach or play with her on the floor at the same time. The three of them became three BFFs.

The four of us became a close-knit family unit. I never worried about Kelsey when she was in the house or backyard because I knew the dogs were not letting her out of their sight. Every time Kelsey came home from school or an activity, she would immediately look for her dogs and the dogs would be waiting for her. They were fiercely protective and loyal to us.

These dogs were more than just our friends and family members. They actually protected us. We both felt safe knowing that they were with us. On one occasion, Izzie even got between Kelsey and a huge rattlesnake that was in our backyard. I will never forget Izzie's bloodcurdling screams as she valiantly fought the snake that kept lunging at her and Kelsey. She fought the snake to the death and probably saved Kelsey's life that day.

On another occasion, I heard the dogs barking in the middle of the night and raised the garage door and looked outside with a flashlight. Out of the corner of my eye, I saw what looked like a bear running across our front lawn from our trash cans. It scared me to death, but I think our dogs' barking scared it away. I should note that bear sightings are not that rare in my neighborhood. Home security cameras have caught pictures of bears rummaging through trash cans in our neighborhood. Remember, we are adjacent to the Oaky Woods Wildlife Management Area, and that habitat continues to get smaller as new subdivisions are being built in the area.

Within the last couple of months, our neighborhood has had numerous home burglaries and automobiles vandalized. A few weeks ago, I had fallen asleep in the den and was awakened by strange noises after midnight. I could hear several male voices talking to each other, and it sounded as if they were trying to manually lift our garage door. I was frightened and peered out the side window to try to see what was going on. The dogs immediately started barking ferociously, and the strangers ran away down the driveway.

I believe our dogs would have done anything they could to protect us. Neither of them had any type of special training, but they seemed to instinctively know what we needed. I am a diabetic and, on occasion, my blood sugar will get dangerously low. One night, Sadie woke me up by barking and licking my face. She had sensed that something

Figure 36 The three best friends watching TV

was wrong with me. When I woke, I was shaking, dizzy, and sweating. I realized that my blood sugar was low, and I needed to immediately eat or drink something with sugar in it. I tried to get up and felt the room spinning. I told Sadie that I needed Kelsey's candy. The dogs were always watching Kelsey eat, and they especially liked to eat her treats when she left them laying on the coffee table or on the counter. Sadie left the room and returned a few minutes later with a half-eaten bag of Gummy bears for me to eat. After eating a few of them, I was able to raise my blood sugar level and feel better.

These are just a few examples of how our dogs loved and cared for us. We felt happier and safer when they were with us. We thought we would spend at least the next ten years with our fur babies. I dreaded the day that they would become old and die. I thought that would be unbearable.

*****

Figure 37 Kelsey is an animal rights advocate Photo credit: Bonnie Rebholz

Wednesday, October 3, 2017, started out as a typical school day. My alarm went off at 5:30 a.m. so I could wake Kelsey up at 5:45 a.m. to get ready for school. As she did every morning, the first thing Kelsey did was take the dogs outside into the backyard and feed them. As I had to do every morning, I called her in from the back-yard and told her she had to say good-bye to the dogs because it was time to eat breakfast and get ready for school. She gave the dogs their daily morning hug and told them that she would tell them all about her school day when she returned home that afternoon. When the school bus picked her up at 6:50 a.m., she was happy and eager to start her school day.

The dogs played in the backyard that morning, enjoying chas-ing squirrels and rabbits. Everything seemed so very normal and serene. At 9 a.m., I was in the shower getting ready for work when I thought I heard a loud banging on my front door. I turned off the water and heard another loud banging noise. It startled me and I slipped getting out of the shower and fell (the strength and balance in my legs were not yet fully recovered from a recent hospital stay). I almost panicked and was scared that there was some sort of emergency at my front door. I struggled to pull myself up off the floor and throw on some clothes. I rely on a walker to be able to walk, and I slowly moved as fast as possible given the circumstances. By the time I was able to get to the front door, I encountered two angry animal control officers from the county. They had two large official county vehicles with flashing lights in front of my house. I must admit I was scared to death to see this spectacle in my front yard.

One of the officers asked me if I was the owner of two dogs. I said yes and he proceeded to tell me that they had a complaint that there were two large vicious dogs roaming the neighborhood scaring families who were afraid to leave their homes. I was speechless and in a state of shock to think that he was referring to Sadie and Izzie. Just then, I heard them barking at my neighbor's dogs on the side of my house. I told the officers to wait a minute, and I went to my side garage door. I opened the garage door and found Sadie and Izzie in our driveway barking at the neighbor's dogs (who were behind a wrought-iron fence in their yard). The neighbor's dogs were also agitated and barking at my dogs. I yelled, "Sadie and Izzie." When they heard their names, they ran like lightning bolts into our garage and into the house with me.

I returned to the front door and informed the officers that the dogs were now in the house, and I did not know how they had gotten out of the backyard. One of the officers told me that one of my neighbors had videoed the dogs jumping over our fence, and they had acted viciously toward him. He proceeded to inform me that this was not the first time this had happened, and the neighbor had complained to them on previous occasions. I listened and let the words sink in. Then I asked him why no one had ever called me about this. They said that no one had my telephone number, and they had no way of contacting me. I told them that this was obviously not true. My neighbors had my telephone number, and the county even had my number. I am on their emergency alert system and the county is constantly notifying me of any impending storm and emergency situations.

I also told him that they had just seen how easy it was for me to call the dogs back into the house. When my dogs had gotten out on previous occasions, they had become upset when they could not figure out how to get back into the backyard. Usually, they dug holes under the fence to get out and explore. I have previously spent thousands of dollars on paying someone to install an invisible fence (three times), which the dogs subsequently figured out a way to chew the wires and chew off each other's security collars. I also spent thousands of dollars on paying my lawn service company to put bricks, chicken wire, and even concrete at the base of my fence to cover all holes and other places they are likely to dig. During the last five years, we have responsibly taken every possible step to keep our dogs secure and safe in our backyard.

The other interesting fact is that I understand that Izzie can jump. In fact, one of her favorite pastimes is jumping on the trampoline with Kelsey. Sadie, on the other hand, is smaller and doesn't jump. She is even scared to go upstairs, so we have to carry her up and down the stairs. I can't imagine her easily jumping over a six-foot fence. No one has shown me the video that allegedly exists showing them both jumping over the fence. Furthermore, our backyard fence has three heavy-duty security locks that stay locked almost all of the time (including the morning of the incident). It is true, when I called them in the house, they somehow had managed to get out into the driveway. It would have been helpful if someone could have adequately explained how they got there.

The other peculiar fact about this sudden concern about "vicious" dogs roaming the neighborhood is that dogs accidentally get out of yards in our neighborhood on a frequent basis. The neighborhood association's Facebook page is full of posts with pictures of over seventy-five dogs that have been found in other people's yards during the past year. In fact, a few days before, we had found a strange dog in our driveway who was barking at our dogs in the backyard who were subsequently barking back at him. Instead of calling 9-1-1 to report a "vicious" dog in the neighborhood, I posted his picture on the neighborhood association's Facebook page asking if anyone knew who this dog belonged to. This is what good neighbors do for each other.

I was shaking with anger to think that anyone in my neighborhood would sit and wait until my dogs supposedly jumped the fence so they could videotape them and subsequently call 9-1-1 to tell them that "vicious" dogs were roaming the neighborhood without a leash. I apologized for my dogs getting out of the back yard, and told the officers that I would try to make certain that they did not do it again. They said that was not good enough. He gave me two citations for not restraining my animals and a notice to appear in court later that month. They also informed me to not let the dogs out of the house until this situation was resolved. I attempted to explain to the officers that this was part of a bigger issue that was not about the dogs, and they did not want to hear about it. It is ironic because I am fairly confident that few, if any, of the owners of the other seventy-five dogs that were found roaming unleashed in my neighborhood were given a citation, court appearance order, and a several-hundred-dollar fine. It is significant that the family of a small autistic child with intellectual disabilities is the one family who was singled out to suffer negative consequences when the other incidents were ignored.

After the officers left, I went back into the house and locked the door. A couple of days prior to this incident, we had received an anonymous note left in our mailbox. The poorly worded message warned us that we needed to be careful because anything could happen to our dogs. The ominous warning implied that our dogs were not safe. I must admit that we have many wonderful neighbors, but I was aware that one or more of my neighbors did not like the fact that a family with a special needs child is living in the neighborhood. Apparently, they feel that they do not want to see a special needs child with intellectual disabilities happily playing with her dogs in the front yard when they drive by our house. In their minds, this scene is bad for home property values.

I began to shake in fear for my child and her dogs. I realized during the encounter with the officers that whoever was targeting my child and her dogs was not going to stop. This was an orchestrated attempt to drive us out of the neighborhood, and that was just a matter of time before the dogs would accidentally get out of the yard again. I was afraid that they eventually would be either poisoned or shot by these people who seemed so determined to get rid of us. I was even more afraid of my child being hurt in the process. It was my duty to protect them, even if it meant our dogs needed to be somewhere safe without us. I cried for over an hour at the injustice of this situation that was treating our beloved pets as collateral damage. However, this had been our home for over thirteen years, and we could not afford to move. I know that our situation is not unique. Discrimination against the developmentally disabled is far too common in our country, and our neighborhood is just another example of this unjust and ugly reality for far too many special needs children and their families.

I called the director of the Flint Humane Society and told her about our situation. Kelsey has been a big supporter of that organization and has collected over six thousand pounds of dog food donations (over three tons) for them. She also designated them to receive a donation check for five thousand dollars when she won the National Prudential Spirit of Community award earlier that year. We knew they did great work and cared deeply about animals. After hearing our plight, the director told me to bring Sadie and Izzie to them. She said that they would protect them.

Figure 38 Kelsey mourning the loss of her two best friends Photo credit: Bonnie Rebholz

I loaded Izzie and Sadie into the car. They looked at me with trusting eyes knowing that their mommy would protect them. I cried the entire one and a half hour drive to the Flint Humane Society office. The dogs knew something was wrong and tried to kiss me and lick my face while I was driving. It was the saddest and most emotional drive of my life. All I could think about was how I had let them down and failed to protect them. When we arrived at the Flint Humane Society, I took Sadie and Izzie into the lobby. We had a group of volunteers and board members waiting for us. They sat with me and got to know the two dogs who shook their hands with their paws. I was sobbing uncontrollably and did not stop until a little toddler (who was in the lobby with his mother) went up to the "vicious" dogs and kissed and hugged them. That was God's way of telling me that Sadie and Izzie were going to meet new friends who would love and take care of them. The good people at the Flint Humane Society told me that they were going to keep Izzie and Sadie together and they would go home with them that night. I needed to return home to meet Kelsey when the school bus dropped her off after school, so I quietly said goodbye to our fur babies and left the building. I cried all of the way home realizing that I had never cried like this in my entire life.

The worst part of the day was telling Kelsey that she would probably never see her dogs again. She didn't believe me when I first told her the dogs were not in the backyard. She went into the back-yard and called their names. She finally sat on the back porch area next to their food and water bowls and sobbed uncontrollably. She had just lost her best friends and never had the opportunity to say goodbye. It was a rough evening. She didn't want to eat and didn't want to talk about it until after 9 p.m. (when she should have already been asleep). Kelsey asked me why people could be so mean and why God would allow this to happen. I told her that I did not know, but I knew that God loved us and he loved Sadie and Izzie. She took comfort in the fact that Sadie and Izzie were with good people who loved them. However, she cried herself to sleep in my arms.

In the days since that horrible day, Kelsey has been sad and lonely. She attempts to go about her daily routine of school, extra-curricular activities, and community service projects. However, I can sense her quiet despair and sadness. I have contacted our friends at the Flint Humane Society to check on Sadie and Izzie numerous times. They are doing well. The Flint Humane Society has worked with an organization to ensure that they have been adopted and are currently in good situations.

Our attorney feels we did the right thing by attempting to deescalate the situation and keep our dogs safe. Since Sadie and Izzie have been gone, our neighborhood is still not safe. Pets have gone missing with some coming home shot. Others have been found dead. I thank God every night that Sadie and Izzie are safe and have not been injured or killed.

Sadie and Izzie will always be part of our family. A piece of our hearts is missing, and we pray for them every night. The only thing they are guilty of is loving and protecting my daughter. Even though it remains a hostile atmosphere, we are not moving from our neighborhood. Life can be unjust and unfair, especially in a neighborhood not known for its diversity or acceptance. However, I am teaching my daughter that you do not run from bullies. Instead, you stand up to them with kindness and resolve. We pray for those people who are willing to deliberately be cruel and torment children with developmental disabilities and their pets. Perhaps God can help them see the light and become better human beings.

*****

Figure 39 Kelsey and Izzie praying together
Photo credit: Tamara Joiner

In the meantime, Kelsey will continue to be a strong advocate for no-kill animal shelters. She will continue to support the Flint Humane Society and other shelters that are dedicated to protecting innocent animals. We are all God's creatures and we have a responsibility to protect each other.

Almost one year later, in August 2018, a friend of ours contacted us and told us about a small Yorkie named Maggie that needed to find a good home. She said she immediately thought of Kelsey and that she might want another dog. Maggie is a small Yorkie that stays in the house the majority of the day. We were frightened that something might happen to Maggie in our neighborhood but decided we would take the chance and never let her outside the house (including the backyard) without a leash. At first, Kelsey was reluctant to bond with Maggie because she thought she was being disloyal to her memory of Izzie and Sadie. However, when she met sweet Maggie, she fell in love with her and the two have become inseparable.

Figure 40 Kelsey and Maggie in August 2018

Unfortunately, the negative behavior toward the developmentally disabled in our neighborhood has not ended. On Easter of this year (April 21, 2019), Kelsey got on her bike to ride two miles around the neighborhood in her effort to raise money and awareness for the HALO Group. The organization is in the process of establishing life skills and vocational opportunities for young adults with developmental disabilities in middle Georgia.

As of Easter Sunday, she had proudly ridden her bike 210 miles toward her goal of 250 miles by the last day of school (May 24). She loves to stop at the neighborhood pond every day to sit on one of the benches and watch the mother geese and babies swim across the pond. I do not worry about her being around water because she knows not to get into the water and she is a competitive swimmer on the Warner Robins Aquanauts Swim Team competing in five events (freestyle, backstroke, breaststroke, butterfly, and individual medley).

Easter Sunday, however, the ugliness and bitterness of the world came to our doorstep. Kelsey came home with a police officer following her. The polite and kind police officer told me that they had received an anonymous complaint from one of our neighbors about a developmentally disabled child riding her bike in the neighborhood. Apparently, the neighbor does not feel that my fifteen-year-old daughter has the right to ride on public streets and sit by the community pond because she is autistic. The police officer apologized but wanted to let me know that someone had complained about Kelsey. I asked him if Kelsey had done anything

wrong and he said absolutely not. He said he followed her home and she stopped at every stop sign and looked both ways and stayed on the side of the road while riding her bike. He reaffirmed that Kelsey has the right to ride her bike and that he could not give me the name of the neighbor who complained because it was an anonymous call, but he thought I needed to know. I thanked him for telling me.

I have always been reluctant to pursue litigation; however, enough is enough. I have an obligation as Kelsey's mother to protect her and every other developmental disabled child. My daughter is a fifteen-year-old honor roll student. She has every right to exercise and enjoy riding her bike (or even walking) in our neighborhood.

Figure 51 Grand Marshall of the 2019 Journey Ride for Autism

*****

God must be watching over Kelsey. Central Georgia Autism (a nonprofit family advocacy group) saw a story on social media about what happened to Kelsey while she was attempting to ride her bike in her neighborhood. They selected her to serve as the grand marshal of the 7th Annual Journey Ride for Autism Bike Race benefiting the families served by Central Georgia Autism's scholarship program. On May 4, 2019, Kelsey, with the US Air Force Cycling Team, led the pack of bike riders from the starting line. Over two hundred bike riders from throughout Georgia rode the twenty-two-, thirty-three-, sixty-six-, or hundred-mile course that covered three counties. We are grateful for Central Georgia Autism for giving Kelsey this wonderful opportunity to support a great cause and help teach the community a valuable lesson about kindness, compassion, and inclusion.

Also, in early 2019, I was approached by a group of my neighbors asking me to run for the subdivision's homeowners association board. They wanted someone who would represent the silent majority of the neighborhood who are concerned and disgusted regarding all the negativity and mean-spirited behavior that has been going on in the neighborhood (especially on our street) for the last several years. They cited want happened to our dogs as one example. They also cited examples of some of the homeowners routinely posting very negative and nasty messages on the homeowners association's Facebook page, some of which include derogatory racial remarks as well as sarcastic remarks about "special education." In addition, at least one post used the R-word when referring to local residents with developmental disabilities. I will never understand what is missing in someone's unhappy personal life to cause him/her to continually post negative comments about other people on social media. They are an embarrassment to the wonderful people who live in our neighborhood.

With my neighbors' encouragement, I agreed to run for a position on the board. I was elected and am serving as the homeowners' association board secretary. I take Kelsey with me to every monthly meeting and I hope that our quiet presence is helping, in some small way, to create a more accepting, inclusive, and appropriate family-friendly environment in the neighborhood.

CHAPTER 9

Pageants

I am obviously not a pageant person. In the first fifty years of my life, I had never been to a pageant and had no interest in watching pageants. One day, in 2014, Kelsey was reading the local paper and saw an article, written by Alline Kent, about a local pageant for special needs girls. Kelsey said that she wanted to do that. The annual special needs pageant had just been held and would not be held again until the following year, so I told Kelsey that I had seen in the paper that the Miss Warner Robins Pageant was going to be held in a few weeks and I would take her to watch it. A few weeks later, we did not know what to expect when we drove to the civic center to watch the Miss Warner Robins Pageant. We watched the younger girls compete in the afternoon and the teens and older contestants compete in the evening.

Kelsey was fascinated watching the girls walk across the stage in the beautiful pageant dresses. She asked me if she could go on the stage and walk with them. I did not realize that the people sitting behind us at the civic center could hear our discussion. I looked around behind us and saw Pam (her dance teacher) and her daughter, Meredith. Pam told me that she did not realize Kelsey was interested in pageants. Both Pam and Meredith had competed in pageants and they both knew Kelsey well. Pam asked me if I would consider allowing her to informally help Kelsey learn more about pageants. She said it might be a great developmental activity for Kelsey. I said yes because Kelsey was obviously very excited about the idea. At that point, I had no idea just how much of an impact pageants were going to have on Kelsey's life.

That day, we watched Kelsey Hollis be crowned Miss Warner Robins Outstanding Teen and Betty Cantrell be crowned Miss Warner Robins. The next summer, Betty Cantrell would go on to be crowned Miss Georgia and, subsequently, Miss America. Also, during the next summer, Kelsey Hollis would ask Kelsey to serve as her princess during the Miss Georgia Outstanding Teen competition in Columbus.

Kelsey Hollis took a big chance on asking a developmentally disabled child with autism to be her princess and go on stage with her during the Miss Georgia Outstanding Teen Pageant. No contestant had ever done this before, and if my Kelsey had not handled the lights and the crowd while on stage, it could have negatively impacted Kelsey Hollis's chances of winning. Fortunately, everything went great while they were on stage. My Kelsey loved every minute of the time she was able to spend with Kelsey Hollis during the competition. In fact, my Kelsey also served as Kelsey Hollis's princess for the next year at the Miss Georgia Outstanding Teen competition and

Figure 41 Kelsey at the Miss America Outstanding Teen Pageant in Orlando in August 2016

was present the night Kelsey Hollis was crowned Miss Georgia Outstanding Teen. My Kelsey subsequently traveled with Kelsey Hollis to Orlando to the National Miss America Outstanding Teen competition to represent Georgia as a National Princess in August

2016. During the competition, my Kelsey received the Top Princess Fundraiser in the Nation Award for the Children's Miracle Network Hospitals from the Miss America Outstanding (MAO) Teen Organization. We will be forever grateful to Kelsey Hollis and her mother for giving my Kelsey the chance to experience this once-in-a-lifetime opportunity.

Kelsey's pageant career really began the day after the Miss Warner Robins competition in July 2014. I did not have a clue about where to buy a pageant dress, what type of hair and makeup Kelsey needed, how to train Kelsey to walk on stage, and how

Figure 43 Kelsey's first pageant in September 2014

to train her to actually speak on stage or during an interview, etc. Her dance teacher, Pam, patiently gave us free expert advice. Kelsey had been attending dance classes at KidsAmerica in Perry since she was three years old, and Pam knew Kelsey and how to work with her. She had always been a tremendous role model and positive influence on Kelsey's life. Because she knew Kelsey so well, she knew her strengths and weaknesses.

Figure 42 Miss Georgia Cinderella Teen at the Georgia National Fair Parade in October 2018

I found a relatively inexpensive purple dress on the internet and, after Pam told me it would be perfect for Kelsey, I bought it. Pam allowed Kelsey to come to the dance studio after hours and practice walking on stage. Pam also taught her the importance of maintaining eye contact with the judges. This is a very difficult skill for a child with autism to perfect, but Kelsey kept practicing until it seemed second nature to her. Pam also gave us advice on the type of questions Kelsey would have to be able to answer from the panel of judges. This was a very difficult task for Kelsey because of her developmentally delayed communication skills. Pam even wrote Kelsey's onstage introduction that Kelsey memorized and continues to use five years later when she competes in pageants.

We were very nervous, but we entered Kelsey in her first pageant competition on September 27, 2014, at the Miss Bleckley County Forestry Pageant. I did not know what to expect. The best thing about pageants from my perspective is that the contestants' mothers (i.e., me) get to be in the dressing room with the contestants to help get them ready and give them support and guidance. As girls get older, so many activities require the parents to drop their daughter off at the activity and pick them up when it is over. In pageants, mothers are expected to be there supporting their daughters every step of the way. I like and can support that philosophy. I will never forget that evening. I walked with Kelsey from the dressing room and was ready to walk with her backstage before the competition started. Kelsey looked at me and said, "The other girls' mothers are sitting in the audience. I want to be like the other girls." Then she kissed my cheek and told me she could do this. I was never so proud of her, but I was worried because she had never walked on stage during a pageant competition. That night was phenomenal. Kelsey had a megawatt smile the entire time she was on stage. She looked graceful as she walked across the stage, maintaining perfect eye contact with each judge. To my shock and amazement, at the end of the night, she won the pageant in her age division and was crowned Junior Miss Bleckley County Forestry.

During the last five years, Kelsey has gone on to compete in over a hundred pageants and win at least fifty pageant titles. Many of these pageants were benefit pageants that supported terrific causes such as Shriners Hospitals for Children, Children's Miracle Network Hospitals, St. Jude Children's Research Hospital, Children's Healthcare of Atlanta, Ronald McDonald House, Georgia Empty Stocking Fund, Flint Humane Society, Autism Speaks, CARES (cancer victims) support fund, Susan G. Komen Foundation, Breast Cancer Research Foundation, American Cancer Society and Crime Stoppers.

Figure 44 Pageant Talent Competition in August 2018

Because of her disabilities and very small size, Kelsey does not look or act like the stereotypical pageant contestant. On stage, she looks tiny. Often she is at least one foot shorter than any of the other contestants in her age group. At fifteen years old, Kelsey is only four feet and eight inches tall. This means that Kelsey does not often win the top beauty title at pageants. However, Kelsey is a strong competitor for any community service-related title. Most importantly, however, Kelsey's communication and social skills keep improving dramatically in every pageant she is in. Kelsey is not at these pageants primarily to win the beauty title. She is there to continue to overcome her developmental disabilities by improving her communication and social skills. Each time she competes, she is competing to be better than the last time she competed. This is why I try to screen the pageant systems she competes in to make certain that they are willing to allow her to continue to grow in a nurturing, accepting, and inclusive environment. The vast majority of pageant directors, contestants, and mothers we have met have been kind, considerate, and understanding. We have met many fine people through pageantry.

Some of the pageants Kelsey competed in required a talent competition. Once again, Pam volunteered to teach Kelsey tap and jazz talent routines that she could perform during the competitions. After serving as her dance teacher for several years, Pam expertly choreographs routines that are entertaining and can showcase Kelsey's personality.

I could spend the entire book talking about all of the wonderful pageant experiences we have had, but I would be misleading if I also did not mention some of the mistakes and missteps we have made in our pageantry journey.

After the first year, I realized that we were asking Pam to volunteer too much of her time for free to help Kelsey. I offered to pay her to be Kelsey's pageant coach. She declined. She offered to continue to help in any way she could and continue to coach Kelsey for her talent routine, but she did not want to start officially coaching pageant contestants. So I started paying Pam to give Kelsey private lessons to improve her talent dance routine and looked for someone to serve as her pageant coach. I found someone who was considered to be a good coach, and it worked out well for a while as long as Kelsey kept winning pageants.

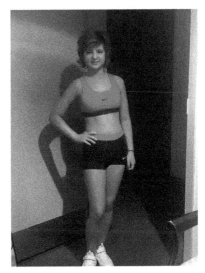

Figure 45 Waiting to compete in fitness routine at a MAO OT preliminary pageant

However, in the fall of 2017, I decided to allow Kelsey to start competing in the Miss Georgia Outstanding Teen (MAO OT) preliminary competitions. We knew this would be a steep learning curve for Kelsey because, at thirteen, she physically looked like she was a ten-year-old and was probably at least a foot and a half shorter than any other contestant. She was four feet eight inches tall and only eighty pounds. Kelsey was also only in the seventh grade, and the vast majority of the other contestants were in high school. We traveled throughout Georgia for Kelsey to compete in six preliminary Miss Georgia Outstanding Teen competitions that season. She improved dramatically by working hard and practicing every day. Unfortunately, she did not win a title in any of the competitions. She did, however, meet many beautiful and talented new friends during the preliminary pageants. It was a wonderful experience for Kelsey.

Kelsey was excited when she won an award and a $275 scholarship at one of the MAO OT preliminary competitions. Unfortunately, Kelsey and the other five participants who won scholarships that evening never received their scholarship money. When the girls contacted the Miss Georgia organization to ask them to give them their scholarship money, they were instructed to contact the Miss America national organization to ask for it because it was not the responsibility of the Miss Georgia organization to ensure that they received it. The Miss America national organization instructed the girls to file an official grievance with their organization so they could officially investigate the matter. They also told the girls that they were not responsible for ensuring that they received their scholarship money. It is a sad commentary for an organization that considers itself a scholarship competition. The truth is that some of the competitors who win scholarships do not actually ever receive their scholarship money.

By competing that year, Kelsey sharpened her stage, talent, fitness, and interview skills. However, the most important thing that Kelsey gained that season was her voice. She began to understand the important role she is playing in promoting inclusion and the acceptance of diversity. During the last couple months of that preliminary pageant season, she received over two hundred private messages, texts, and even letters from girls with developmental disabilities and their parents from throughout the United States. They told her that she is an inspiration to them and an example of how anything is possible if you are willing to work hard and never give up.

While Kelsey was competing and losing, I noticed that her pageant coach was getting harder and harder to reach. She did not show up for any of Kelsey's competitions and slowly stopped returning my text messages. For a year, I sent her text messages requesting that she call me or schedule a coaching session with Kelsey. Usually, she would reply to my text saying she was busy, and she would contact us in a few days. We never heard from her. She did, however, post politically correct words of encouragement on Facebook for the pageant community to read and pretended to be actively involved in Kelsey's pageant career.

Kelsey had to compete in the Miss Georgia OT preliminary competitions with no coaching advice (other than talent and fitness routine advice from Pam) and no expert support (other than Facebook friends expressing encouragement). It broke my heart to see her coach abandoning her because she was no longer considered a "winner." After Kelsey had not had a coaching session with her for over one year, I sent her a

Figure 46 Interview with judges' panel at a MAO preliminary pageant Photo credit: Bonnie Rebholz

text message requesting a phone call with her to discuss why we had not heard from her despite my repeated attempts to contact her. She responded by sending me a text saying she had no record of me texting her and that she was busy and she would contact us later in the week. We waited two additional months to hear from her and then finally ended our affiliation with her when she did not contact us.

We learned a valuable lesson during this experience. Kelsey's heart was broken because she thought that this individual loved and cared about her. My heart broke watching my child be hurt by someone she loved and trusted. I realized that not everyone is who they pretend to be. It is politically correct to talk about how you want each girl to live up to her own potential and find her own inner strength and beauty. However, some pageant coaches are only interested in winning and being associated with girls who are capable of winning major pageant titles.

This story has a happy ending because we have found another pageant coach, Anna Barnes, who is considered one of the best in the business, and has been kind and supportive of Kelsey during these past several years even when she wasn't Kelsey coach. Kelsey needs positive role models in her life and it is my job, as her mother, to make certain we find them.

I am contacted frequently by mothers who have daughters with disabilities asking for advice and guidance about pageants and whether or not their daughter should be involved. I tell them that before allowing your daughter to participate in any pageant, you need to thoroughly research the pageant system. You need to make certain the system and the pageant director are nurturing, supportive, and promote kindness and an inclusive environment. You also need to stay away from pageant systems that have a documented track record of financially exploiting their contestants. Countless research studies have documented that individuals with disabilities are much more likely to be exploited than the general population in this country, and pageants are no exception.

Figure 47 America's Elite Miss National Ambassadors in January 2017
Photo credit: Photography by Frank Carnaggio

A good example of a great national pageant system is the America's Elite Miss. In 2017, Kelsey was crowned one of their National Ambassadors. In 2018, she was crowned a Legacy Ambassador, and in 2019, she was crowned their National Role Model. The system, directed by Kerrie Juliana, is known for encouraging their queens to be kind, dedicated, compassionate, and fierce! They stress community service and value it highly. Kelsey has met many lifelong friends and role models through this system.

In our case, almost all of the pageant systems that Kelsey has participated in have been wonderful. However, I would not be truthful if I said that we have not had bad experiences. One of these experiences has been particularly painful for Kelsey.

Kelsey competed in her first international pageant competition in July 2015, when she was eleven years old. When she won the Georgia state beauty title for that pageant system, she became eligible to represent Georgia at their international competition in Dallas. It was an intimidating challenge considering Kelsey had been competing in pageants for less than one year at that point. We knew that this pageant had a mandatory talent competition and that the other competitors were going to be some of the best ten-to-twelve-year-old dancers and singers in the nation. Most of the dancers had already won national dance competitions, and some of the singers already had professional recording contracts. Many of these talented young ladies had talent agents and were performing professionally. We knew Kelsey had never been in competition dance and her skill level would never be in the same ballpark as the other contestants. I worried that Kelsey would not be accepted and would feel out of place and overwhelmed. On the other hand, I did not want Kelsey to miss out on an opportunity to reach for the stars and experience this level of competition. I prayed a great deal about it and decided to let Kelsey go to Dallas to compete with the most beautiful and talented girls in the country.

July 2015 was probably one of the best months of Kelsey's life. From the minute she checked in until the time we left, Kelsey was welcomed with open arms. The other contestants encouraged and supported her. They cheered for her and encouraged her to be the best she could be. Kelsey had never performed on a professional stage like the one at the Eisemann Center for the Performing Arts. She handled it like a pro and had a megawatt smile on her face the entire week. While she obviously did not have the same skills as the other contestants, she was treated as an equal and felt like she was just one of the girls. This was an amazing experience for a child who had been sitting in a self-contained special education classroom with other special education students for several years. Of course, no one expected Kelsey to win any major beauty or talent awards, and she did not. However, to our surprise and amazement, Kelsey was awarded the pageant's Spirit Award for possessing inner beauty and the true meaning or "spirit" of the program. The night she won the award, she held on to that plaque as if she had just won the Academy Award. I have never seen her so excited.

Figure 47 Pageant talent competition in July 2015

For the next two years, in July 2016 and July 2017, Kelsey returned to compete in the international pageant and had amazing experiences. We traveled to Dallas each year knowing we were not going there to win anything. Instead, we were going to be able to spend one week interacting with a group of wonderful, kind, and compassionate girls from all over the country. They made Kelsey feel welcome and part of their group. They also cheered for Kelsey during all phases of the competition (interview, talent, beauty and onstage introduction), gave her advice, and most importantly, were her friends. Kelsey would look forward each year to making this trip and would talk about it constantly after we returned home.

The trip in July 2017 was particularly challenging for us. I had only been out of the hospital for a few months and was still recovering from being in a coma for four weeks. I had not yet regained full use of my legs and could barely walk using a walker. In addition, I was starting to lose almost all of my hair and did not recognize the person I saw in the mirror. I had told Kelsey in June that I did not know if we could go on the trip because I needed to recover more to be able to drive us to Dallas. I worked hard all of June and July at the physical therapy center to regain as much strength as possible. Despite doctors' advice not to go, I loaded us, all of Kelsey's pageant wardrobe, and my walker in our Ford Mustang and we headed for Dallas. It was a long two-day trip. When we stopped for gas or lunch, Kelsey had to get out of the car first and unload my walker and bring it to my car door. Each time, I struggled to get out of the car and walk the few steps necessary to either get gas or buy lunch for Kelsey at a fast-food restaurant. However, we made it safely to and from Dallas. It is amazing what you can accomplish with determination and God and Kelsey as your copilots.

Because of Kelsey's wonderful experiences the previous three years, we thought the international pageant competition held in July 2018 was going to be terrific. We could not have been more wrong. That year, the pageant system reorganized and appointed a new state pageant director for Georgia. For whatever reason, she made Kelsey's life miserable. In the summer of 2018, I had still not gained full use of my legs and was having other health issues resulting from my hospital stay. My doctors again discouraged me from traveling to Dallas. However, Kelsey had been looking forward to this trip all year and wanted to see all of her friends. For Kelsey's sake, I again loaded us, all of Kelsey's pageant wardrobe, and my walker in our Ford Mustang and we headed for Dallas. It was a long two-day trip that exhausted me. I could barely walk with the assistance of my walker into the hotel lobby after we arrived in Dallas. Once we arrived in our room, I had to unpack and begin to iron all of Kelsey's pageant clothes.

Once we arrived at the pageant, the bullying started. I will never understand why, but the state pageant director and a small group of mothers new to the pageant system decided that they wanted to belittle, mock, and humiliate my daughter. I suspect that they were insecure and jealous of how nice everyone was to Kelsey and thought it would be easy to make themselves look superior by going after a tiny developmentally disabled child. I also suspect that they thought I was too weak and feeble to stand up for my daughter.

Most of the bullying was so petty. For example, I paid the state director twenty-five dollars in March so Kelsey could have a warm-up jacket and pants to match the other girls from her states. She kept telling me that she was going to mail it to me before July and never got around to mailing it. Once we were in Dallas, she kept putting me off about it while posting pictures of the other girls wearing their jackets. She also kept giving me excuses why she could not find Kelsey's crown, but she promised she would give it to her while we were in Dallas and never did.

The worst thing they did was continuing to talk about Kelsey and exclude her from their activities during the entire week we were in Dallas. At the parties, they would stand in a little group looking at Kelsey like she was a subhuman and openly talking about her. It got so bad that, at one point, a mother from another state whom I did not know, sat down next to me and apologized for their behavior. She said that it was obvious to everyone that they did not like Kelsey, and they were making fun of her disabilities. She said the mothers were acting like immature middle-school mean girls who enjoyed bullying girls who were different than them. The next day, when I was in the dressing room waiting for Kelsey to finish competing, another mother (whom I did not know) entered the dressing room and introduced herself. She said that her daughter who was competing had a sibling who was developmentally disabled. She started to cry with me and hugged me and told me that she understood.

I had several other mothers approach me during that week to express their support, tell me about someone in their life who was disabled, and told me to keep my head up and do not allow them to crush Kelsey's spirit. I will never understand what is missing in someone's character that would make them behave in this manner toward Kelsey or any other developmentally disabled individual.

Kelsey did not allow them to negatively influence her performance at internationals. Kelsey was nervous competing that year because she moved up into the teenage division. She was an incoming seventh grade developmentally disabled student who was competing with teen girls, some of whom had just graduated from high school with honors. The hardest part of the competition for Kelsey was the expanded onstage introduction. Kelsey rehearsed hours each week that summer in order to be able to deliver her introduction flawlessly on stage. She used the introduction Pam had originally written for her when Kelsey started competing in pageants. It captured her soul and her personality and was perfect for Kelsey. The best part of the competition that year was the support Kelsey received from the other teen contestants. They surrounded her with love and support. They encouraged her when they thought she was nervous or unsure of herself and even walked with her in the hallways outside of the dressing rooms as she was waiting for her turn to go on stage. We will never forget their kindness and support when she needed a friend that week. To our surprise, at the end of the pageant during the awards banquet, Kelsey received the pageant's Spirit Award for the fourth year in a row. Needless to say, we were thrilled!

Unfortunately, the bullying situation did not improve after we left Dallas. The state director and small group of mothers continued to bully Kelsey on social media with sarcastic remarks. The state director never gave Kelsey her state crown despite my repeated inquiries. After I asked her about it more than five times, I found Kelsey's old state crown (which was identical to the one she should have received), dusted it off, and told her to wear it proudly. I could have pulled Kelsey out of the pageant system at that time, but I wanted to turn this unfortunate situation into a teachable moment. Kelsey had earned the right to represent her title for the remainder of the year, and she was not going to quit just because some bullies did not like her. I told her that she was going to finish the year representing her title by making appearances at charity events and helping with community service projects, and then we were going to quietly walk away from the drama with our heads held high.

They continued to do petty things like deliberately scheduling their Christmas party on the day they knew Kelsey had promised to attend a Christmas party for children with developmental disabilities. The other state-title holders all received a Christmas present from the state director and she posted a picture of them at their party and expressed how much she loved the other girls in the Facebook post. This type of pettiness lasted all year, and it made Kelsey miserable. She was treated as a subhuman by these individuals, which is an obvious example of discrimination against the developmentally disabled.

Because of this experience, this particular pageant system has lost its luster for us. No pageant system should allow or tolerate this type of unprofessional and unethical behavior. I kept my receipts for the money that I paid for the warm-up suit and the crown. I have been advised to turn them into PayPal to report potential fraudulent activity. However, I chose not to do this because I am tired of the drama surrounding these individuals. Instead, we chose to pray for them. We hope God shines light into their hearts and teaches them how to become better human beings.

CHAPTER 10

Community Service Projects

As a mother, there is no greater joy than to introduce Kelsey to the concept of God and how he wants all of us to help others and treat them as we wish to be treated. I have spent my entire professional career working for and supporting organizations that help people. I wanted Kelsey to learn at an early age about the joy and satisfaction that comes from helping others.

I have been the prekindergarten Sunday school teacher at my church for the past thirteen years. I enjoy teaching my four-year-old students about our faith and subsequently watching them develop into responsible teenagers. For the last several years, Kelsey has volunteered with me every Sunday morning as an aide in my Sunday school class.

Figure 50 First Communion ceremony at Sacred Heart Church

Kelsey started working on community service projects when she was six years old. When Kelsey was in first grade, we self-published a two-volume collection of short stories about her daily life. In 2011, we traveled throughout Georgia as part of her statewide book tour speaking to a variety of audiences involving individuals ranging in age from toddlers to senior citizens. At each event, Kelsey read a book to the audience and subsequently shared a copy of one of her own books while answering questions from the audience about her life.

*****

In late 2018, Kelsey used the interview and onstage speaking skills she developed through pageantry when she applied to be a volunteer advocacy ambassador with Autism Speaks. She got the job and is currently serving as a Georgia Autism Speaks volunteer advocacy ambassador. The international autism advocacy organization is headquartered in New York City. Kelsey's responsibilities include establishing and maintaining relationships with federal legislators; serving as a media stakeholder and liaison; recruiting other volunteers to participate in autism advocacy; working directly with Autism Speaks staff, both in Atlanta and Washington, DC, to implement advocacy initiatives; and being involved in autism-related meetings/events.

Through this position, Kelsey is working with the other state Autism Speaks volunteer advocacy ambassadors to help millions of Americans who are on the autism spectrum and their families. She worked for months with them to promote the passage of the Autism CARES Act of 2019 in the US House of Representatives and Senate. The Autism CARES Act authorizes $1.8 billion dollars in federal funding for autism research, services, training, and monitoring.

Kelsey also worked with Georgia Governor Brian Kemp's staff to develop an official proclamation that was signed by Governor Kemp declaring April 2019 as Autism Awareness Month in Georgia. She worked with the Houston County Commissioners and the Mayor and City Council of Warner Robins to have similar proclamations for the county and city.

Kelsey is currently serving as a junior advisory board member for the nonprofit HALO Group. The organization is in the process of establishing vocational and life skills training opportunities for young adults with developmental disabilities in middle Georgia. Kelsey has participated in numerous fundraising and awareness activities for the organization. To date (July 28, 2019), she has jogged, biked, and swam for 397 miles since January 1, 2019 toward her new goal of seven hundred miles by December 31, 2019. She is earning one dollar per mile for the HALO Group for every mile she makes. I admire her determination and grit to log in her miles on a daily basis while she attempts to make this goal.

Figure 52 Receiving Proclamation From Georgia Governor Brian Kemp in April 2019

Kelsey is also currently serving as the local coordinator for Houston County Adventure Bags Project. The project works with local organizations that work with displaced children (i.e., DFCS, homeless shelters, domestic violence shelters, teen shelters, etc.) to give the child a book bag filled with important items like a tooth brush, toothpaste, shampoo, conditioner, hairbrush, comb, soap/body wash, washcloth/puff, socks, a coloring book, crayons, sippy cup, bottle, pacifier, bib, baby wash, baby washcloth, dia-

Figure 53 Raising funds and awareness for the HALO Group

pers, wipes, blanket, a stuffed animal to hold, or a journal to write down their thoughts with so that when they do have to go to an unfamiliar place they have something to call all their own. Bags are filled age-specific from infant to eighteen years old, male and female.

Figure 54 Buying food to donate to the Houston County Backpack Buddies Program

Figure 55 Facilitating a workshop at the National School -Based Health Alliance Conference in Indianapolis

In addition, Kelsey is currently serving as the special needs ambassador and advocate for the South Georgia Regional Prevention Coalition (six county rural regional coalition). Kelsey's responsibilities include collecting donated school health clinic supplies and educational outreach materials and speaking at community outreach events.

Kelsey is also a big supporter of no-kill animal shelters. She collects donations for the Flint Humane Society. Since May 2015, she has donated over 6,900 pounds (three tons) of dog food to the organization. The Flint Humane Society helped us by find good homes for Izzie and Sadie when we needed their help during the crisis situation in our neighborhood. We know firsthand the important role they play and want to support them in any way possible. Some of the proceeds from Kelsey's second book, *A Girl and Her Dogs,"* are being donated to them.

Because of Kelsey's humble start in life, she knows what it is like to be malnourished and starve. This is why she continues to collect food donations for the Houston County Backpack Buddies Program. The

122

program provides nutritious weekend food for local hungry and malnourished students. Since May 2015, Kelsey has donated over 3,500 cans and boxes of food for the project.

Kelsey has also written several grant proposals totaling over twenty-five thousand dollars to fund autism awareness outreach materials, school health clinic supplies, nutritious food, and sports equipment for economically deprived children.

She has raised over thirty thousand dollars for a variety of charitable organizations including, but not limited to, Children's Miracle Network Hospitals, Shriners Children's Hospitals, St. Jude's Children's Research Hospital, Children's Healthcare of Atlanta, Ronald McDonald House, Georgia Empty Stocking Fund, Flint Humane Society, Autism Speaks, Wounded Warrior Foundation, Tattnall County CARES (cancer victims) support fund, Susan G. Komen Foundation, Breast Cancer Research Foundation, American Cancer Society, and Crime Stoppers.

I am very proud of the fact that Kelsey is currently serving as an intern for Norris Consulting Group. Her responsibilities include researching potential grant funding opportunities that will help support local community service projects and assisting with developing a training program to teach young

Figure 56 Developed "Everyone Belongs" curriculum for middle and high school students

people (ten- to eighteen-year-olds) how to write grant proposals and obtain other financial resources to fund their community service projects. I have enjoyed teaching Kelsey these skills and helping her teach others.

In 2018, Kelsey facilitated resource development workshops targeting youth throughout Georgia and at the national School-Based Health Alliance conference in Indianapolis, where she trained 150 youth leaders from throughout the nation.

Figure 57 At a book signing event

In 2019, Kelsey and I worked hard to refine her original workshop material to develop a new curriculum for middle- and high-school-age youth leaders. It is called Everyone Belongs. It teaches empathy, compassion, inclusion, and community service skills. It will also teach young leaders how to write small grant proposals to fund some of their community service projects that help others in their community.

Kelsey and I have also collaborated by coauthoring two books. The first book, *I Want to Make a Difference,* stresses the importance of community service and never giving up. The second book, *A Girl and Her Dogs,* stresses the importance of compassion, tolerance, and acceptance. We have found a joy in sharing our life experiences with others. Because of these books, we have been invited to give motivational presentations at schools, workshops, and conferences. We love sharing our message of focusing on trying hard, never giving up, and achieving your dreams.

Kelsey has received letters of encouragement, about our books, from people like First Lady Melania Trump, former first lady Laura Bush, former Georgia first lady Sandra Deal, Georgia state school superintendent Richard Woods, and former president Jimmy Carter, who wrote, "I am pleased to learn of your new life in the United States, the incredible challenges you have overcome, and your love for serving others. You are in inspiration to friends of all ages around the world."

All of the community service work has added up to over 3,500 documented volunteer community service hours for Kelsey. Kelsey is the recipient of the prestigious 2018 International "Yes I Can!" Award from the Council for Exceptional Children (professional organization for special education teachers). She has also been named the 2017 Georgia Top Middle School Volunteer and one of the Top 10 Youth Volunteers in the Nation by the National Prudential Spirit of Community Awards. Kelsey is one of the youngest children in the country to have received *two* awards from the Kohl's Kids Care Scholarship Program, which recognizes young people who make a difference in their community. She has also received the gold president's volunteer service award *six*_times with congratulatory letters from

Figure 58 At the Council for Exceptional Children's Annual Conference in Tampa in spring of 2018

presidents Barack Obama and Donald Trump. In addition, she has received official resolutions from Georgia governor Nathan Deal, the Georgia State Senate, and the Georgia House of Representatives, commending her for her work to support Georgia children who are in crisis and in other difficult circumstances.

Figure 59 Talking to Olympic Gold Medal Swimmer, Michael Phelps

Fortunately, I have been able to attend her award ceremonies with one notable exception. When Kelsey was selected as Georgia's 2017 Top Middle School Volunteer, she was invited to attend the award ceremony in Washington, DC, in May 2017. She was excited and we were planning the trip. In March 2017, I collapsed and was in the hospital for four weeks on a ventilator in the ICU in critical condition. No one expected me to live but, through God's goodness and grace, I survived. When I came home in April, I could still not move my legs and was receiving dialysis treatments.

One of the first questions that I asked my doctors when I came out of my coma was whether or not I would be well enough to take Kelsey to Washington for her awards ceremony. My doctors just laughed and said, "I think you will need to make other arrangements." Thankfully, Kelsey's dance teacher and mentor, Pam, volunteered to chaperone Kelsey and travel with her to Washington, DC. It was an exciting trip for them. The top middle and high school youth volunteers for all fifty states were invited to attend the conference and awards ceremony. This award is sponsored by the Prudential Spirit of Community Initiative and is the most prestigious volunteer award that a middle and high school student can receive.

During the trip, Kelsey got to meet one of her heroes, Olympic gold medal swimmer Michael Phelps. He encouraged her to keep swimming competitively and told her to give his best wishes to her Warner Robins Aquanauts teammates. Kelsey also visited the offices of Georgia senators Johnny Isakson and David Perdue to talk about the importance of community service and how youth can make a difference in their communities. The highlight of the trip, however, was when she met with United States secretary of agriculture, Sonny Perdue, who is a former Georgia governor and Bonaire native.

All of these middle and high school youths were considered by a judges' panel who selected five middle school students and five high school students to be included in the 2017 Top 10 Youth Volunteers in the Nation. Because the awards luncheon was streamed live, I was able to watch Kelsey receive her award from the rented hospital bed at my home while I was waiting to be transported via nonemergency ambulance for my outpatient dialysis treatments.

Figure 60 Top 10 Youth Volunteers in the Nation, Prudential Spirit of Community Initiative

I will never forget that day. The ambulance personnel had arrived to transport me and I asked them to wait because they were in the middle of announcing the winners' names. When Kelsey's name was announced and she came to the podium, the ambulance staff (who had never met Kelsey) were cheering with me as we watched Kelsey receive her award. They gave me a high five and seemed just as excited as I was. We all started crying when Kelsey came to the podium to accept her award. No one thought Kelsey would win and would have to give a speech, so we did not practice anything before she left for Washington. She calmly walked to the microphone and thanked everyone for her award. She then thanked Pam who took time off from work to travel with her to Washington. She told the audience that I was very sick and could not be there and asked them to pray for me.

Their prayers must have worked. Two years later, Kelsey and I are still going strong. Life is good. We are blessed. Needless to say, I am proud of the young lady Kelsey is becoming. Of all of her accomplishments, I am the proudest of her community service activities. We are put on this earth to help others. We all have different skill sets and abilities. It is our responsibility to use our skills and abilities to help others when we can.

CHAPTER 11

Future Plans

Early in 2019, I was notified that I had been selected as the 2019 Georgia Mother of the Year by the American Mothers, Inc. This annual honor is awarded to a mother who exemplifies in her life and conduct the precepts of the golden rule and the power of a mother's inner strength to deal with the successes and challenges

Figure 61 January 2019
Photo credit: Heather Ray

in life. She should also exhibit an interest in her community by participation in programs and services that enrich mothers, children, and families.

I was shocked and humbled to receive this honor. We flew to Washington, DC, in April 2019 to accept this award and meet with congressional and senate leaders to discuss issues of importance to Georgia families. During the awards ceremony, I had to give a speech. I thought it would be appropriate to share it in our book. The following is the transcript of my speech:

I struggled during the past several weeks to prepare this speech. As Georgia's 2019 Mother of the Year, I am supposed to talk about issues that are important to Georgia's mothers. There are so many serious issues facing Georgia's families. I have spent my entire professional career (over thirty years) working to help children and families in Georgia. During that time, I have interviewed and facilitated focus groups with thousands of parents. I have interviewed parents across the state who have seriously ill and, even, ventilator-dependent children. I have even interviewed parents who had children who had passed away during the previous week. I thought I understood what it was like to be a parent and the issues they faced. I was mistaken. I didn't realize what it meant to be a parent until, at age forty-two, I decided to adopt a special needs orphan. I didn't realize what it is like to watch your heart walk out the door every time she leaves for school or leaves to ride her bike in the neighborhood. I certainly did not know what the daily challenges and barriers parents of special needs children face.

The amazing thing that I have learned as a mother of a special needs child is that there are wonderful people in this world who are willing to step forward with encouragement and support. I am not a politician and don't usually use the phrase "It takes a village"; however, Kelsey is where she is today because of the "village" of people who have supported us. This includes our friends, teachers, babysitters, coaches, doctors, dentists, speech and physical therapists, neighbors, church family, and Kelsey's pageant family. Raising a special needs child requires a strong parent who is willing to love her unconditionally. A parent needs a strong support system of terrific human beings. It is especially important when you are a single parent.

For every "bad apple" who crosses your path, you are going to find hundreds of other kind, decent people who are willing to be supportive. Children with special needs can be successful and make a difference in this world. They just need the right support and guidance from adult role models. Kelsey and I have been fortunate enough to have this support and we are very grateful.

—Carol Norris
Acceptance speech given at the American
Mothers Annual Convention
April 2019

This spring, I was elected to the state board of directors for Parent to Parent of Georgia. Parent to Parent of Georgia offers a variety of services to Georgia families impacted by disabilities or special health care needs. These are Georgia's Parent Training Information Center, Family to Family Health Information Center, Babies Can't Wait Central Directory, Parent to Parent USA State Affiliate, and the Region 8 Parent Technical Assistance Center. Each year, Parent to Parent of Georgia assists thousands of Georgia's families. I feel strongly about the need for this organization. Parents need advocates, and I am honored to be able to support this essential organization.

It is critical that this nation embraces individuals with disabilities. While many people have talked about this issue, we believe in the importance of self-advocacy for individuals with disabilities. Individuals with disabilities and their families live, eat, breathe, and sleep with our disabilities every day of our lives. No one can fully understand what it is like to have a disability unless you actually have one or have a family member with one. We intend to continue to demonstrate that individuals with disabilities can achieve great things in life and make a tremendous difference in the lives of others.

Specifically, we will continue to help others (especially children and struggling families) to make certain that every child in a crisis situation receives the assistance they need. That means helping children who are taken out of their homes with nothing but the clothes they are wearing, go to school hungry knowing that their school lunch is the only meal they are going to eat all day, go to school sick because their parents cannot afford to take them to see a doctor, and have no clean clothes to wear. Kelsey has spent the last several years volunteering for over 3,500 documented community service hours to address these issues, and I have served with her for every one of the 3,500 hours.

We are proud of the lives we have led and want to continue to help people. I will continue to serve my clients as president and senior consultant at Norris Consulting Group. We are also continuing to write books, teach workshops, and give motivational presentations. We are working toward establishing our own foundation in the next couple of years that will support individuals with disabilities and children who are in crisis situations. This is the legacy that we want to leave behind. Life is short and we thank God every day for allowing us to be on this planet for another day.

ABOUT THE AUTHOR

Carol Norris is the 2019 Georgia Mother of the Year. For more than thirty years, Carol has served as a devoted advocate for nonprofit organizations, public agencies, and community collaboratives that serve children and families. Carol Norris is the president and senior consultant of Norris Consulting Group. The company is recognized as one of the leading consultants (specializing in health—, social service—, and education-related projects) in the United States. Carol has written over three hundred successfully funded grant proposals totaling over $153 million to fund after-school programs, school-based health centers, juvenile delinquency prevention programs, mental health services, child health networks, school wellness programs, and other family support programs. These services have subsequently assisted hundreds of thousands of poor and disadvantaged children and families.

Carol currently resides in Bonaire, Georgia, with her fifteen-year-old daughter, Kelsey. She adopted Kelsey as a single mother, from a Russian orphanage when she was fourteen months old. Kelsey is currently a nationally recognized advocate, community volunteer, beauty queen, author, and athlete. She has been diagnosed with having autism, intellectual disabilities, and Rubenstein-Taybi syndrome. Kelsey believes that individuals with disabilities can achieve great things in life and make a tremendous positive difference in the lives of others. When she grows up, she wants to be a role model for others and start her own charitable foundation that will support individuals with disabilities and children who are in crisis situations. Carol and Kelsey have coauthored three books and are in the process of writing additional ones.